Confessions of
a Concierge

Confessions of a Concierge

a Concierge

Madame Lucie's History of
Twentieth-Century France

BONNIE G. SMITH

YALE UNIVERSITY PRESS
New Haven and London

Library of Congress Cataloging in Publication Data

Smith, Bonnie G., 1940–
Confessions of a concierge.

Includes index.
1. Lucie, Madame.   2. France—Social life and customs—
20th century.   3. France—Biography.   I. Title.
CT1018.L83S65   1985   944.08   84–27032

ISBN: 978-0-300-04038-8

For

Mary Anne
Rachel
Bill

J'ai plus de souvenirs que si j'avais mille ans.
BAUDELAIRE

Contents

Introduction:

Telling Common Lives

Whose history should we write and how should we write it? These are questions that historians must confront at least indirectly as they practice their craft. The problem of whose voices to listen to and how to interpret them underlies all written literature. Struck by George Eliot's astuteness and realism in describing common lives, Henry James wondered how, after her creations, one could ever write satisfactory history. A century later historians are still wondering how to emulate the richness and humanity of fictional narrative. In addition they must justify, as novelists need not, their choice of topic. Even conventional choices of kings, wars, or diplomatic missions are not taken for granted; one must start by explaining not only the life but the choice. This is especially true when the subject is not famous, but obscure—not a powerful man, but a poor woman; not a king, but a concierge. So Henry James posed only part of the problem at hand when he asked, "How do we write history?" We must further explore not only that question but why one might be interested in the subject of our story: a Parisian concierge named Madame Lucie.

Many people have, of course, found concierges fascinating and their power mysterious. In urban France this power derived from a combination of roles: collecting rent, learning and telling secrets, guarding keys and things locked away by keys, informing and refusing to inform police—by acting, in short, as majordomos of the small communities formed by apartment houses. Into the concierge's purview came scandals, blackmail and blackguardism, love affairs, and crimes reaching even to murder. For sheer dramatic possibilities the story of a concierge like Mme Lucie is attractive. As a representative of her occupational group, she could open a window on social history in general through her own access to French ways of life. In that case, however, Mme Lucie might fade into the type she represents and into the more familiar denizens of French society, especially the Parisians—fascinating, fashionable, always making revolutions and strikes, always in the twentieth-century avant-garde. This collapsing of the particular into the general has recently made historians more interested in hitherto unlikely candidates for historical narrative—the miner, the immigrant, and even the concierge.

Yet it was Mme Lucie as an individual who first captured my attention. Over the years this woman fascinated both the neighbors who relied on her and strangers from around the world who happened onto her *loge*. The latter have corresponded with her, sent her novels they have written, or simply kept in touch. One novelist, hearing that I was about to do this biography, was both crestfallen and enthusiastic. A great topic, he thought; a great story, he added, but more in his line of work than mine. Such women of the people—the Becky Sharps or those who carried old wives' tales—were best handled by novelists whose métier was just this delineation of character and private lives. What, my friend asked, was all this business of subjecting Mme Lucie to the dreariness of historical narrative? What business did a historian have telling not great lives, but common ones? The "who" and "how" of historical writing were posed again from a different perspective.

One could, and perhaps should, turn the question around.

Introduction: Telling Common Lives

How did novelists for so long virtually monopolize so many good stories—those of tradespeople, lovers, adventurers, ladies of leisure, and concierges? For centuries historians typically wrote about popes, kings, and warriors, along with wars, depressions, and class struggles. Taking the high road of public visibility (or "significance") in their choice of topic, historians secured their claims to distinction by the reliability of their professional apparatus—source material often confined to written records, footnotes, bibliography, and the like. They generally opted for a way of telling that limited their subject matter to men and women of public importance and to attendant public events that meshed with this Plutarchian mode. Tellers of "great" lives have probably been professionally satisfied, for they have provided proper documentation while also narrating a human story and indulging any penchant for drama or melodrama. By cleaving to the stature of their subject, such biographers could survive the descent into mundane, daily life with reputation intact. By contrast, it was the novelist who eschewed derivative grandeur and learned display, and developed instead the techniques for telling common lives—dialogue, symbols, flashbacks, stream of consciousness, and dozens of others—that created interest in the ordinary, even humdrum lives of people played out in the private world, far from the historical stage. The significance of this world relied on the novelist's skill in the telling, not on the status of the protagonist. So traditionally historians focused on the "who," whereas novelists based their claims on the "how."

Given this orthodoxy, my novelist friend was perhaps right. Madame Lucie—her love life, her work life, her small intrigues and those of her neighbors—belonged to fiction and not to history. Like a shell in the sand or a wave on the ocean, she fascinated rather than dominated. Or one could say that in contrast to Napoleon or Madame de Staël, who dominated vast areas of experience, she dominated but the tiniest corner: her family, about forty tenant families and artisans, and occasionally a police officer who wandered too close to the people she protected. Yet the historian should not surrender her so easily to fiction. For one thing, Mme Lucie talked with me about World War II, the depression, Princess Grace of Monaco, and François Mitterrand. How could a historian resist stories of Coco Chanel, the world wars, and Saint Theresa the Little Flower, whose childhood home had been just around the corner from Mme Lucie's boutique in Lisieux?

Madame Lucie in fact possessed a century of such stories about French life, and anyone interested in history could hardly ignore them. After all, history has always been a world of memory to be recaptured by reflection and by explaining life through storytelling. Madame Lucie was at home in this world of storytelling, and she gave the impression of being an experienced, though not a trained, historian. Certainly she was an expert in spinning tales, as I learned from our earliest encounters in 1971. On my departure from Paris that first summer spent in her building, we stood, concierge and tenant, for a final conversation—and one that extended beyond the greetings we normally exchanged in those early days. Breaking the usual French reserve, Madame Lucie asked how old I was. When I replied, she gallantly avowed that I didn't look my age.

"And how old do you think I am?" she continued. Madame Lucie looked, in fact, incredibly old but responded that she was only seventy-five. She took my surprise as admiration for her youthful appearance and then recklessly proceeded, "Have you, Madame, perhaps made a baby in Paris this summer?" Always handing out bits of information, Mme Lucie was actually trading it for more precious coin—the new facts she then put on file for some unforeseen occasion.

Soon thereafter my family settled in Mme Lucie's building for several years. She took us on and took us in. As foreigners the problems we generated and those we experienced were both larger and smaller than those of her French tenants. As foreigners we were also susceptible to the seductions, charms, and beguilements of our hosts; we received comfort from the smallest courtesies and attention. Madame Lucie offered all those in abundance, even when, after returning to the United States, I saw her only summers. Although her friendliness grew over time, it still remains a bit mysterious. Was it merely the facade of a shopkeeper's daughter or something more insistent? In any case, when we were thus fortuitously brought together during the next decade, Mme Lucie, Rapunzel-like, unloosed the thick coil of accumulated memories. Anecdotes, as R.W.B. Lewis said of Silone's peasants, became her form of communion.

This communion, these anecdotes, and these memories turned into Mme Lucie's history of twentieth-century France. Gregarious but lonely (for reasons that will become clear later), she spun out her tales like a born *raconteuse* who delighted in a daily audience. At times she seemed to serve no other master than the one who inspires all such spinners, concerned only to interest her audience—in my case, a lover of history. At other moments, insistently, she became my Ancient Mariner, forcing me to serve her need to descant. In both moods Mme Lucie would occasionally pause after a succession of memories to explain her longwindedness: she rambled on, she said, to tell me the true "history of France." One had to admit that all the ingredients were right—she touched on most of the major events and personalities of the century.

Certainly, too, Mme Lucie's experience fit with all the statistics and almost every generalization about twentieth-century France. An only child, who had two children herself, she seemed in accord with the French tendency to limit fertility. Her parents were tradespeople who went out of business in World War I. Madame Lucie married beneath her partly because of the shortage of suitable husbands at the end of that conflict. Then she and her family migrated in search of jobs and ended up in the Paris region, where the new car industry provided employment for her husband. Made homeless during World War II, she became a concierge to solve their housing problem—a problem faced by many during the apartment shortage of the postwar years. In all this, one had new justifications for telling her story. Madame Lucie was indeed common in the way that has attracted social historians. How interesting for once to see life behind the statistic, to see the stigma of divorce in operation, to watch generational changes and the perception of changes in such an important city as Paris. In Mme Lucie's story the past became humanized in a way that social history aspires to but often fails to achieve.

Despite this fidelity to the official record or her ability to enrich it, Mme Lucie's self-proclaimed status as historian remained troublesome. She was no Fernand Braudel, had no education, and certainly had no official records. More than that, her way of telling was naive, especially when one considered that most professional historians have sophisticated ideas about psychoanalysis, social contexts, or quantitative methods. Her own character formed during the *belle époque*, Mme Lucie told her tales with the certainty of a nineteenth-century novelist who knows good from evil, heroes from villains. Instead of detachment one found value judgments; instead of mental subtlety, a direct approach to what she considered important in the French past. All in all, Mme Lucie seemed too close to her tale to meet standards aspired to by unbiased social science.

Moreover, what Mme Lucie considered important rang with heterodoxy. She would discuss war and depressions in the same breath with the Provençal method of washing baby diapers, thus distorting the normal arrangement of significant events. Certainly the texture was richer than most histories. Her tales of Queen Navalo, the garrison at Lisieux, and the little train connecting coastal resort towns in fact brought to mind that great pursuer of memories Marcel Proust, for whom the events of French history constituted a backdrop for that same Queen Navalo, the same little train, and the Lisieux garrison. For him, remembering the quotidian was heavily laden with universal import when it connected with the narrative artistry of literature. But still, one had to admit again that Mme Lucie was not Proust, who cloaked his elegant memoir in intensely learned (or intensely vapid) conversations, in uncommon obsessions, and in an uncommon beauty beyond the reach of the likes of an old concierge. Lacking such artistic genius, Mme Lucie's insertion of the commonplace into the record of the past violated the canon that historical narrative for the most part must tell of significant events, public deeds, and glorious people.

Madame Lucie was not a historian because she retold the past from a perspective that broke too many rules. Unlike most historians, Mme Lucie looked from *within* French society at events occurring outside her circle. This point of view, this window on the past, inverted the normal historical narrative written by an outsider looking at people and events. In so observing, the professional historian often filters out those moments, occurrences, or stories that seem unimportant (because common), but that may in fact have held profound significance for "commoners" like Mme Lucie. So too her perspective differed from that of the movers and shakers, the makers of wars and economic conditions, who write memoirs. Yet it is precisely this insider's perspective that should encourage us to treasure Mme Lucie's history. Because her vision was undistorted by the spectacles of the professional historian or the powerful diarist, Mme Lucie's story was a testimonial, an exhibition of that *mentalité* scholars seem to invoke the more they cannot recapture it.

There was a time (wasn't there?) when a good deal of history was told in this way, when grandmothers and grandfathers could recite generations of family or local history. There was a time, too, when villages might have sages who performed a similar telling function or when people wrestled to put their lives, the lives of their friends and family, in some kind of perspective vis-à-vis the larger events around them. One's history was a form of confession based on sober reflection on the past and its multiple layers of personal, familial, and public experience. Madame Lucie's ruminations belong to a narrative tradition that few dare to uphold in the face of the professional historian's expertise. In most professional eyes, only what is public—the ups and downs of politics, the cycles of economics or masses of statistics—is worth consistently writing about. With history as this drums-and-trumpets account, the "confession" has become merely personal, sentimental, melodramatic—the "true confession." Madame Lucie's tale revives a telling of lives that can still be satisfying. At the very least, this long-lived woman lets us in on a rich and multifaceted way of telling that has almost been lost with the professionalized methods of analyzing (and often oversimplifying) a complex past. In this respect Mme Lucie's tale is doubly historical as it looks back on the past from an outmoded perspective—that of the amateur, the bard, the *raconteuse*.

About fifty years ago American intellectuals began the quest for testimonies of the likes of Mme Lucie's. In this search for the lost or disappearing people of the American past, writers—often from political and intellectual left—developed what today is called oral history. Oral historians have found and recorded narratives of slaves, of sharecroppers, immigrants, and union members. It was and still is seen as a rescue mission to retrieve the inarticulate, to preserve their quaint ways threatened with eradication by mass culture, and to find out how the working people of America feel or felt about their experience. In all this, the accent was on the common, without much interest in the telling—either in the narrative structure or in the matter of intrinsic historical import. Most oral historians saw their subjects as "common" men and women whose stories were being heroically rescued. Conscious of his or her importance in historical reconstruction, the oral historian was going to save American "authenticity" and in so doing perform a political act by mounting evidence of modern cultural destructiveness. In addition, the oral historian often agonized at great length about his or her role or class position vis-à-vis these commoners. The debates over methodology and the correct position of the historian toward unfortunates of other classes sometimes dominated the oral history itself.

In other words, the subjects of oral history were items on the political agenda of intellectuals. Oral historians sought out ex-slaves and miners from a pre-established commitment. But there exist other paths to historical meaning. In the case of Mme Lucie quite the reverse occurred: she was as far removed from my historical agenda as possible. Her narrative demands on my time interrupted the progress of my other work, and the meanings she suggested were at that particular moment largely gratuitous—the product not of the public and analytical history I practiced but of the private stage on which she played out her life. She presented herself, often insistently, sometimes coyly, as she used her historical facility to hold her audience in place, keeping her company. Madame Lucie again inverted the present historical scheme of things not just by inverting point of view. She also presented herself as a bit of historical seren-dipity, totally nonutilitarian as, in a way, all life is; as, in a way, all history is.

Madame Lucie's life poses as many questions as it answers because of the intractable nature of human experience; her life demonstrates why historical writing can never be exclusively theoretical, why the questions "who" and "how" must con-stantly be reopened. Like Mme Lucie, each individual can at any moment mess up all theory or disturb our answers.

By giving this book an eccentric form I have tried to recap-ture a few of the multiple ways history may appear to us and to suggest the range of relations individuals may have to the past. This introduction, for example, presents different theo-ries about women's, working-class, and French history that I hope will provoke the reader to generalizations about Mme Lucie's life. In Part I Mme Lucie offers her life to us in an autobiographical mode, which I have actually pieced together from the higgledy-piggledy order in which she told her story. This autobiographical mode aims to revive Mme Lucie's voice and point of view by using her words while reordering her narrative through the historical convention of chronology. Part II imitates the order of Mme Lucie's memory, the order of her daily life in later years, and the order of observations made about her by many witnesses. This "true" account employs such fictional techniques as dialogue (but these dialogues did occur), a third-person and omniscient narrator, and flashbacks. If the reader wants, he or she may also pay attention to the ways in which Mme Lucie distorts, throughout, what might be considered normal, historical time by interjecting feelings, stretching moments that are important to her, breaking her narrative. Such were the methods used to recreate the fictions and histories that developed in her uncommon endeavor (which extended over more than a decade) of making life whole by restoring it to memory and to speech.

Through this experiment I hope to suggest the multiple perspectives and multiple genres that work to construct our vision of the past. Anyone's past can accommodate abstractions, narratives, and critical points of view. The reader may conclude that Mme Lucie becomes but a vehicle for such an experiment to bring the student to a more rigorous appreciation of the varieties of history. But I hope that although Mme Lucie serves that purpose, she will also illustrate our theories and simultaneously refute them with her individual search for communion with others and with history. Hers was a common life, full of rebellion, unhappiness, love, acceptance, and, at the end, a waiting for death and the great silence. The storytelling effort—her gift to us—represents a unique human and historical superfluity in this age of standardization. Or is it the other way around? Do we all have stories to tell—stories whose circulation is the basis of our communion? Despite our apparent absorption in a monolithic, impersonal, and national culture, perhaps we are (like Mme Lucie) at the same time tribal, village-like, and resistant to our homogenization by professional interpreters. Perhaps, too, it is what seems common—our individual rebellions, unhappiness, and the way we suffer births and deaths—that constitutes a unique bravery demanding more historical import than is usually credited.

Whatever the answer, we turn to history because it tells us about lives, about living, and about living *in history*. Our curiosity about individual lives, about the lives of groups, and about the great collective life in which we all participate as citizens turns us to the past. There we find thwarted lives, daring lives, powerful lives, and completed lives—like that of Mme Lucie, who begins lost as a child, her character still unformed, and ends in the frailty and fatigue of old age. All these lives are revived in the critical, collective memory we call history. Madame Lucie's life shows how "official" history can distort collective memory when it focuses only on public events and public spaces like battlefields and houses of parliament, the stock market and the factory. It shows too how official history can distort our sense of time past by giving chapters to presidential regimes and not a page—as Mme Lucie's history does—to childbirth and courtship, to saints' days and drowning cats. In witnessing the complexities of Mme Lucie's memory, we are reminded of how complex our histories must be in order to represent richly and fully our collective lives—those of men and women who, like Mme Lucie, have lived valiantly.

Madame Lucie's *Confessions* makes no claim to be a new model for historical writing or for historical sensibility. Though an experiment, this story in fact shares with conventional history the desire to record, to instruct, to amuse, and to question; and it echoes recent requests for human proportions in our appreciation of the past. Where this book departs from others is in its amalgamation of narrative forms—an amalgamation that expresses a specific situation that may not arise for other historians. As the protagonist in William Wharton's *Scumbler* puts it: "When I paint anybody else, we're jammed close: model, me, easel; a triangle, knees touching, wrapped into each other around my paint box" (p. 15). A similar triangle arose in the development of this story, and so its triangular shape tries to express the triangular tenses (present, past, and past perfect) and the triangular perspective (subject, historian, and history) that inform it. Though the resulting form appears a minor rebellion against the historical narrative canon, it cuts a parallel to the firm set of Mme Lucie's jaw as she, for example, sneaked off to find herself a husband or when she rebelled against public officials in protecting her tenants. Other writers may never deal with such rebelliousness or such resistance, nor such particular and personal visions of the past. One refuses to prescribe for them. It is enough to be a minia-turist, especially when one believes—again, like Wharton's *Scumbler*—that in the portrait a triangular past is recaptured and an individual life begins.

Part I
Madame Lucie's Story

1

La Belle Epoque in Normandy

Often, when nighttime fell, my parents had trouble finding me. Returning from work, Papa would search the rooms and when that failed enter the parlor where women were trying on hats.

In those days my mother ran a millinery business in our house. Papa would motion to her. But even though a sign from my father usually called for immediate attention, Maman had other things on her mind when customers were present. Suppose a peasant woman were there, in from the country with all her egg money. She might have seen a hat in our window, and it might have struck her fancy. Entering the house, she would receive the full honors and courtesy of a queen. Maman would shower her with hats, concentrate all energy on studying the effect. She would admire the woman, who probably wasn't used to such praise. In those moments there was little time for Papa, no matter what his mission.

While he stood there impatiently, Maman would adjust the slant of a feather. The customer might hesitate, and then my mother showed her full ability.

"Why, Madame, you are right to hesitate," she would say, scrutinizing the scene. "This hat needs another ribbon." And quickly removing the hat, she would sweep it off to the back room for a rapid adjustment. Papa, of course, would follow.

"It's eight o'clock now, Marie," he pressed for her attention. "Where is the child?" Papa always tried to be stern in my mother's domain. Strewn with feathers, ribbons, and lengths of straw, the workroom where they negotiated disarmed him. Maman continued winding the ribbon; she was in charge here.

A few years before, my parents had met in similar surroundings. Maman had been an apprentice then, winding ribbons and sewing lace on hats in a huge workroom filled with girls and young women. It was the fanciest and largest millinery establishment in the city. One day, when a gas outlet needed repair, the owner called the best plumbing establishment—my grandfather's—for help. Sent to do the job, my father (he was not of course my father then) looked stern as he set about work. But in truth he was lighthearted, loving tricks—and probably never more than in a setting filled with young women and their paraphernalia. What fun, he thought, to play a prank here. So having fixed the outlet, but still crawling around on the floor, he attached one of his tools to the ribbon papers dangling from this table and that workbench. With one movement, he sent the reels of ribbon flying in a cyclone around the girls. The resulting shrieks and laughter made him look up into the chaos, and there he caught the lovely eyes of my mother.

But tonight neither one was laughing and neither had time for tricks.

"You have no idea where she is?" he repeated.

"It's Friday, Victor. The farmers were here all day, the place is full of customers, and you want me to leave them to find Lucie." She used the same words when he complained about simple dinners of chops and steaks: "You want me to leave my customers to make little pastries in the kitchen?"

"Have you seen her since noon?"

"Yes, Victor, she returned around five for *goûter* [snack]."

Untouched by anything but business at hand, Maman returned with the finished hat to the front room.

It was dark, and the soldiers of the Thirty-sixth Regiment were parading through the city by torchlight. As their uniforms filled the streets with twilight color, the people of Caen and the remaining farmers gathered as they did every evening to watch the parade to the garrison, around the church of St. Pierre, up the hill to the citadel. Soon another parade of citizens followed with torches, chanting:

> Ah, the Thirty-sixth Regiment
> With their uniforms so fine and blue
> Marching, Marching to the glory of Caen.

Or they would sing, "C'est la faute d'amour," accompanied by the regimental band.

I was four then, and I sat on the shoulders of the tallest of my grandmother's apprentices to watch the parade. He was so tall that I had a better view than anyone. He always took me home at ten, just as Maman was finising her work.

At four I had my picture taken in a brown and red plaid dress. In our rainy winters it kept me very warm. It was so practical that Maman had me wear it until I was six or seven. Then at five I had another picture taken with Maman. We each had a sausage curl going horizontally across the top of the forehead. She tied mine with a ribbon after rolling the hair around her fingers; her own curl was wrapped and pinned around a piece of mesh to make it stay in place and look more regular. My mother was very beautiful, especially her eyes. But she was also hardworking and strict, as all women were in those times.

We were well-to-do then. Papa had one of two stores in town that sold supplies for plumbing, gas, and electricity. He was among the only men able to do all sorts of mechanical work on plumbing and lighting equipment. So he made the rounds of the hotels, the theater, and the racetrack during the season.

But the Church was his biggest customer, and Caen was a city of churches. Nôtre-Dame de la Gloriette, right by the Palais de Justice, where all the lawyers and important judges worshiped, was our church. For a long time before he married, Papa was master of ceremonies there. To tell the people—who weren't always paying attention—when to kneel and stand, he wore tails and white gloves and had a noise maker to clack at the right time. I remember all the other churches because we learned about them in school. St. Etienne was one, built at the command of William the Conqueror, who was buried there before the Protestants and revolutionaries tore up his grave. His wife Mathilda had St. Gilles built—maybe in rivalry because, as everyone says, she wasn't overjoyed at marrying a bastard. There were many more, including St. Pierre in my grandmother's parish, where I made my first communion.

Grand-mère was a baker, one of the most important in Caen I think. Her bread was wonderful, but I never liked her croissants. So when Maman wanted bread, Grand-mère and I had a little game.

"Lucie, go to your grandmother's," Maman would say. "Get me a small loaf and get a croissant for yourself." She would put two sous in my hand. Off I would go, running the four blocks past the savings bank, by the butcher, then across the street and past the café where the man who had lost a leg in the war of 1870 always leaned and swayed with his red face. Over two more streets and there was the bakery—the house of three corners, it was called because it was triangular, but so big a triangle that the dockers' wagon could go through the double doors into the courtyard.

Grand-mère stood there to watch them unload piles of wood for baking. In those days all bread was made on a wood fire, which gave it a delicious taste. When the dockers had finished, they settled Grand-mère's account, took the roll she offered, and were off to the harbor for another delivery. They worked long hours, those men, but there was one thing I never understood about their families. Dockers' wives always drank a lot and while their husbands were gone would fight among themselves so much that the children—whom I knew, though they weren't our people—were afraid to stay at home. They would come and sit in front of Grand-mère's bakery. When nighttime came, she would tell them to go home, but they always cried. So Grand-mère rounded them up and took them to the police, who never failed to find a place for the poor kids to stay. When their mothers went to collect them in the morning, the police always charged them a sou or two for food and lodging. Well, the dockers' wives were always furious with Grand-mère, but the next day they were soon back, drinking and fighting.

I arrived at the bakery with my two sous. In those days bakers made just bread and brioche, croissants and maybe one other kind of roll. To get cakes or tarts or fancy pastry one went to a dessert place—but not very often, for commercial people like my family knew the value of money and saved for emergencies, for their retirement, or maybe to take a little holiday. If we wanted a treat, however, Grand-mère did have one specialty: pears *bourdaloue*. She wrapped pears in pastry and piled them in a pyramid, four or five on the bottom row, up until there was just one left at the top. The juice and sugar from the top rows dripped down to flavor the pastry all through. I can still remember how good it tasted.

"*Bonjour*, Grand-mère." While I said hello I always looked around the bakery for the pears *bourdaloue*. "Maman would like bread, and a croissant for me, please." I gave her the two sous, and in return she would hand me bread, three sous, and no croissant.

"Thank you, Grand-mère." That was part of our game, but we never talked about it. Grand-mère never had time to talk to me, anyway. She got up early every morning to take bread out to restaurants or cafés, or sometimes my Aunt Suzanne did it before she went off to school. The boys who worked for her kept strange hours, getting up at two or three in the morning to make the first bread. Often they slept while I came on my errands, but at other times I would hide to watch them working almost naked in the heat cast by the ovens. A neighbor woman once saw me peeking like this and told Grand-mère about her wicked little granddaughter.

Because the bakery was right downtown, like Maman's boutique, its clients were shoppers, people leaving mass at St. Pierre's, and, especially, the regiment. Grand-mère supplied the soldiers' canteen. When they went out on a night march, no one in the bakery got much sleep because the man who ran the canteen picked up a load of bread at midnight to follow the soldiers, who would want more snacks than usual. Having made the midnight bread, the boys would just get a couple hours' sleep before the morning bread had to be started.

I always loved holding the three sous in my hand after a visit to Grand-mère, and with them I continued the game by going two more small blocks to her friend, who was also a baker. *Her* croissants I loved.

"*Bonjour, ma petite* Lucie. How is your poor grandmother today?" She always asked the same question.

"She's much better today, thank you, Madame." I learned to say this from Maman.

Grand-mère always dressed in black, and Maman did too for a while because my grandfather died when I was two or three. They said he was young, but I never could understand that because he was forty-seven. In his work, people often died young from "baker's disease" caused by the dust from flour running down the second-story shoot into the mixing pan. Clouds of flour dust like that produced a kind of asthma. Poor Grand-mère, people always said, because even though her business was good now, she and Grand-père had had many misfortunes before finding this prosperous bakery in Caen. And then he died.

"So much the better that she's coming along. Are you going to take a little promenade Sunday?"

"*Oui*, Madame. After Grand-mère goes to mass and does the early morning business, she will leave things with the boys and take a little outing with us and Aunt Suzanne."

My parents loved outings, and maybe that comes from the wanderings of my grandparents. In the 1870s, when Maman was still a baby, they bravely left Grenoble for the north. Grenoble with its mountains and plains is different from Caen, and we in Normandy called people from Grenoble the wolf burners because they used to burn woods around the city, so menacing were the wolves in winter. But I always had a hard time imagining my grandmother, dignified in her black dress, burning wolves.

"Perhaps," the bakerwoman said, "you will go to Trouville and the sea on your little holiday."

She asked me too many questions, and Maman had warned me about people asking questions. But they always thought we went too often to Trouville or Riva-Bella or Ouistreham on the little train—the Décomobile—from Caen. They seemed especially to count our trips to Trouville, where Grand-mère made her first fortune in Normandy.

In Trouville I loved to see all the fancy people walk along the boardwalk, or to watch them get into some kind of machine which pulled them, with all their clothes on, through the water. We never did that, but we waded with our skirts tucked up, or walked the boardwalk in our own very best clothes while Maman got ideas for hats. When my grandparents first came to this area they baked bread for the parents of the very people we saw strolling in all their finery, and in their own shop, too, after Grand-père had saved enough from his job as baker's assistant.

When my grandparents began in Trouville, mostly English

came to the coast, then more French society people started coming—even artists and writers. Planquette was our great writer from Normandy, and it was in Trouville that Mme Planquette made Aunt Suzanne her first little cap. These caps were crocheted and put on babies so that their ears wouldn't stick out.

With all the foreigners, Maman learned to speak English. She taught me to say, "Would you like a cup of tea?" and "I love you." It was also fun to joke with English: the signs in the Décomobile station announced "*Oui*streham" and "*Yes*treham." People in Caen thought it very chic to be like the English of Trouville, and one woman in Caen who wanted to impress Maman invited her for afternoon tea with biscuits and jam. But after living with the English all her childhood, Maman was just bored. Besides, the English were not our kind of people. Maman call them *phlegmatique*. They had no feelings, no sentiment, no sense of passion.

When Madame the baker guessed at Trouville for our outing, I tricked her. "No, Madame, we are going on a picnic." Disappointed, the bakerwoman then suddenly realized, I guess, that she had more important things to do than talk to a child, so she hurried to finish the little game. She would give the croissant I liked so well and take my three sous. One went into the cash drawer for the roll, and two others she put into a little tin. That was my own tin. Every time it was full, the bakerwoman gave it to me to deposit in my savings account. I knew from the beginning of my life that it was good to make little economies and to have a croissant at the same time.

My parents, Maman especially, were thrifty and careful because of what had happened to Grand-père in Trouville. His bakery there prospered so much that he even started a branch in Deauville, which was just beginning to catch attention as a vacation spot. Then, one day, he was ruined. Grandfather, it was said, had made a big loan to a friend he trusted but who left town with a good deal of money.

La Belle Epoque *in Normandy*

My grandparents and Maman moved again to find opportunity in Caen and, I imagine, to escape the scandal. In those days bankruptcy was shameful. Only this time they moved with Aunt Suzanne and two brothers as well, so that Grand-père could start a new life as a baker's helper—at the age of thirty-five! So we didn't go to Trouville or Riva-Bella, because the memories weren't as good as everyone thought.

Sometimes we actually did go on a picnic, a very special kind of picnic that started the night before. When it got dark, my little friends and I would go to the Place Royale and dig worms behind the church. When I had half a pail full I took them home, where Papa and I would sew the worms together in a long string, then wind the string into a huge ball. Next morning—the day of our picnic—Papa and I took the ball of worms and his big blue umbrella made of real whalebone to the Orne River, which ran through Caen and in which the soldiers of the regiment did their washing every week. There we did what is called the *pêche à vermeil*. We threw the *vermeil*—the ball of worms—into the river, and in a second it would attract a dozen conger eels nibbling on it. Quickly we pulled in our catch and trapped them in the open umbrella, which we then closed so that the wriggling eels couldn't escape. We could catch two hundred eels in less than an hour that way, and then we would hurry home to pick up Maman, Grand-mère, and Aunt Suzanne. We piled in a carriage and arrived at a little restaurant in the country where Papa and I in one stroke cut the head and peeled off the skin of each of our catch. For the small price of some eels, the restaurant people fried our eels in butter, mixed them with sorrel, and smothered them with our good Norman cream. And I never did decide which I liked better—a trip to the sea on the little train or eels in Norman cream.

At six I began going to school, and I hated it. Before that life had been an adventure. While my parents worked, I used to wander around the city, or I played hopscotch and diabolo all day in the street, throwing the top up, catching it on the string, up in the air higher, until down it would come. I would never stop playing diabolo in my life, I thought. For three years they were building a savings bank across from my parents' store. All the time the workmen carried the cut stone, I jumped along my hopscotch squares and played at diabolo.

When the Caisse d'Epargne was finally finished, the minister of labor, Monsieur Viviani, came to inaugurate it. Maman had the florist Lami decorate our balcony with rose-colored carnations. We all dressed up and from our balcony had the best view in the world of the ceremony. In spite of all the money that went into the building, however, it was destined to leak from the day it opened, with the little creek behind it sometimes filling the basement right up to the ground floor with water and rats.

School was the end of my hopscotch. It meant sitting on benches while the sisters told you what to do. No talking, a lot of praying, and a lot of work that I didn't do very well. It was an end to my adventures. No more playing in the stream by the Caisse d'Epargne and searching for treasures. No more watching the queen of Madagascar when she stopped overnight in Caen before going to the seashore. Navalo was her name, Queen Navalo, and her arrival was a big event.

"Guess what?" Papa would announce at lunch. "I had some work at the Angleterre today and old Duschesne, the doorman, said that the queen will be coming tomorrow." I would hardly be able to finish my meal before rushing off to tell my friends, Yvonne and Jacques.

Or I would be playing at diabolo when suddenly a whole group of them would come running toward me.

"She's here, she's here."

And knowing immediately what they meant, I would join the race to the Hotel Angleterre, where the queen always stayed. We waited outside, often hiding for the first hour or so for fear of being chased away. Sometimes the wait lasted all day, other times only a short time passed before the queen went for an outing. In either case, we were devoted, and we could always tell when we were about to witness her royal presence. People started coming out doors, carriages would arrive. And while we watched, out would come the queen, always dressed in white. But she, Queen Navalo, was black, black as coal. Every season I would run home to tell Maman about her blackness. I even dreamed about her blackness all covered over with flowing white.

Life before school meant Queen Navalo, diabolo, and mischief. My friends and I used to try to climb the statue of Saint Pierre. Once we even went peepee in the pulpit of the St. Sauveur Church, so far had we strayed from home. After starting school, I realized how bad all these things were. The sisters, especially the oldest, Soeur Geneviève, made me feel my badness, even though they didn't know what I had done. They were so good, and I couldn't be like them anywhere. Particularly in school, I was the bad child. I liked too much to whisper and jump around, and sitting at a desk to write or read was like being in jail.

Perhaps it was different at public school. But I had to be with the sisters because of Papa's business, even though my family wasn't very religious. As I grew older my parents stopped going to mass regularly or fasting during Lent. They had no time for all of that. Besides, people who worked as hard as Maman— from eight in the morning until ten at night—needed their strength. We, however, needed the Church and its business. Papa took care of the chandeliers in every church in Caen and kept the gas outlets in the rectories in good working order. He even went into the convents to fix things, perhaps the only man in Caen who went behind the convent walls. It was a good business, and we were fortunate that Grand-père Brun had found such customers. And also that Papa was so good-humored and clever. He always had a little joke for his clients, or he took an aperitif with them, especially the café and hotel owners. Maman began saying that he did too much of this, but then he could fix anything, install any kind of pipe or duct. Thanks to him we lived in comfort, with running water and toilets like *les grands*. I played my part by going to catechism classes with Monsieur le Curé.

One day Monsieur le Curé told Papa that I was the scandal of the class, that I was a shame to such honorable parents. With my first communion only two weeks away I had been late for mass, having taken a detour on the way. When I arrived at church, the doors were locked. Papa came to walk me home at the end of the services, only to find me sitting and sulking on the steps. He went, furious, to the curé and then had to listen to a lecture about my behavior.

"That man is going to be the ruin of us all," Papa told my mother at lunch. "He talks too much and slanders the government."

Monsieur le Curé had told us that the devil was ruling France, probably because so many religious orders had been denied permission to teach by the government. Even the sisters who ran my school changed to civilian clothes by the time I reached second or third grade. Had they not done away with uniforms, they too, would have had to leave the country. This was what they called separation of Church and State, and Monsieur le Curé never stopped saying that because of the government's policy many people would end up in hell.

"You'll just have to put up with him, Victor," Maman always counseled. It was true that Monsieur le Curè was an influential man who could have ruined Papa's business with just a few words. More than just a society priest as so many were then, he also did much good in the city. In our parish we celebrated his birthday. In fact, prize day at school occurred then: July 21 of every year. Children would write a little poem for him or present him with bouquets. So Maman was correct in bringing Papa round to consider his business duties first.

La Belle Epoque *in Normandy*

Grand-mère was different. Since my grandfather's death, she attended mass many weekdays and always at seven on Sunday mornings. Few of the other merchants did. In spite of all the churches, Caen was more commercial than religious, even though many merchants believed in God and even in the Church.

About the time I took my first communion, Maman sent me to live with Grand-mère. There, she said, I would be closer to school and the cathedral. She also wanted me to run errands, like meeting Aunt Suzanne after work and walking home with her. Aunt Suzanne was about eighteen at the time, and like my mother she sewed like an angel. So when she finished her *brevet* [school-leaving certificate] and apprenticeship, the best lingerie maker in town grabbed her as an assistant.

Aunt Suzanne ended her day at about six or seven in the evening, and I was supposed to wait for her outside the shop. There was often someone else waiting with me—Monsieur Eugène, a soldier in the Caen regiment, and as secretary to the chief of the regimental staff, a very important one at that. When he was there, I followed behind them on the walk home. Sometimes they stopped for tea in his rooms just above the tobacco store, and I had to wait below talking to the two sisters who owned the shop.

Aunt Suzanne hated being in my custody. "Why do I always have to have this little pest for a shadow?" she'd complain. But Grand-mère insisted.

"It's correct to have a chaperone on the streets. I can't do it myself, and I certainly can't send one of the boys."

Actually, I never minded the walks and the waiting. Monsieur Eugène was handsome and dashing, *un beau garçon*, people called him. He had many soldier friends who smiled and winked at us, and I got to see the world as I used to before school came along. Besides, the tobacco shop was very interesting. Often the spinsters' brother was there with all the news he had acquired during the day. As a guard for the Banque de France, in his splendid blue uniform, he made the rounds of businesses, collecting their deposits and their information as well. All the bank guards in Caen were handsomely dressed in uniforms—those of the Crédit Lyonnais even wore a chestnut-colored *casquette* [military-style cap]—and all of them were the best source of news. So I loved the diversion of accompanying Aunt Suzanne.

Sometimes in the spring we had another diversion, when the circus came to Caen. At 9:00 P.M. (for everyone worked until then) Maman closed the shop and put on her finest dress and hat. I did the same, usually having a new outfit to inaugurate. Papa, in his formal wear, admired us grandly. Then we headed for the hippodrome he knew so well. When racing season started, he did a good business there installing phones, lights, and all the other mechanical devices needed. He earned at least ten francs for just an afternoon's work. Of course he did less for the circus because they had their own workmen, but I loved the circus best even though it didn't help our family.

We always started at the main tent where the promenade was, and we joined everyone strolling *en grande toilette*. Maman and I enjoyed this part of the circus because we could see the fashions and hear the news. In other tents one could see lions and their trainer in a red riding habit, as well as clowns and acrobats, and several times they had parrots and parakeets dressed up to represent the marriage of Queen Victoria. My uncle often gave me his tickets to visit the rings, while he sat in one of the chalets where one could take a glass of wine and talk. About midnight we found each other and went home, though I would like to have stayed until the closing at one in the morning. The circus was always magic for me, and when I was young working the next day was no problem.

At the same time as the circus, the dish fair was held in Caen. With both events, the city was flooded with people from the countryside. Everyone came to buy dishes. I mostly went to keep my parents company and to have some french fries and cider at one of the long tables set up for refreshments. Sitting there, I could watch the strange ways of the farmers and their wives—especially the wives. Their manners intrigued me, and so did their clothes.

The peasant women wore dresses very much like German dirndls and white lace hats, the *coiffe*. Some hats were two feet tall, others two feet wide with what looked like wings. Each one was lacy and wrapped in ribbons or embroidered. Maman told me a *coiffe* was very valuable. Once, two sisters near Caen had inherited a *coiffe* from their grandmother and couldn't decide which should have it. So they brought it to Maman's boutique and made her cut it in half. She, too, thought peasants odd and lacking any sense of what to do. On fair days, or even on market days, the conductor of the little train had to round them up like children so they wouldn't miss their ride back to the country. Fortunately, country people are less dull-witted today than they were back then.

Sometime before I finished school we had our family scandal—at least that's what Maman called it. Everyone in our house began talking wildly about Aunt Suzanne and Monsieur Eugène. For several weeks I heard Maman telling my father that something "improper" was going on. Suzanne, she said, knew too much about life.

"Isn't it strange, Victor," she kept saying, "that on Saturday night Eugène sleeps at the bakery, especially when he has his own apartment?"

Papa didn't respond, and my mother grew angry. Her hands were tied, she said, because Suzanne was the favorite. Grand-mère would only scold her older daughter for making accusations against the younger.

Where was the scandal in that? I kept thinking to myself as I tried to figure things out. What was so strange about Monsieur Eugène staying at the bakery, when I did the same thing to keep grandmother company or run errands for her? What could be more romantic than having a handsome soldier around for Sunday dinner?

Actually, it reminded me of the plays and operettas we saw at the theater when the season started. Those evenings we dressed more lavishly than for the circus—even Papa, who accompanied us only to the lobby and then met us when the performance was over. Being responsible for the lighting, he had seen every play more times than we had. *Le Courrier de Lyon, Nôtre-Dame de Paris,* and especially *Les Cloches de Corneville* were my favorites. When I lived in Caen, I could recite almost all of *Les Cloches,* by our Monsieur Planquette. The play that attracted the most attention, however, was *La Porteuse de Pain* [*The Bread Carrier*]. When that ran in town, every baker-woman in the region attended the theater.

In spite of romance, Maman kept up her criticism of our own bread women, and my father continued turning a deaf ear to her pleadings. Then, one weekend, Uncle Jacques, Maman's and Suzanne's brother, came for a visit. I wondered later if my mother had called him in. Everyone in the family looked up to Uncle Jacques, for he had married the daughter of a notary from a village twenty kilometers from town. The wedding had been splendid, with a judge and even residents of a neighboring château in the wedding party. When Uncle Jacques appeared, he too began fuming.

"Eugène arrives Saturday night, mother leaves for mass and her shopping early Sunday morning. You're right, Marie. No matter what is going on, it doesn't look right." That Sunday morning, at 7:00 A.M., he headed for the bakery.

Papa left for the café while Maman and I tended the boutique. She was very quiet, but her beautiful eyes were agitated. When Uncle Jacques stayed away for several hours, Maman grew more and more restless, until he finally burst in.

"I caught them like two birds in a nest."

La Belle Epoque *in Normandy*

Maman quickly sent me upstairs, but listening hard, I could hear almost all of Uncle Jacques's story. He had climbed up the side of the house to the balcony by Suzanne's window.

"I must have looked the fool," he said, angrily, "and all because of my slut of a sister cavorting with a roué." There they were—he could see them from the balcony—like "two birds in a nest," he repeated. He chased Eugène out, made Suzanne get dressed, and waited to confront Grand-mère with proof of the Sunday morning activities at the bakery.

"Wouldn't Suzanne make a great *porteuse de pain?*" he said.

He was furious with her for making him climb foolishly up the side of his own mother's establishment and, he said, for the great dishonor she brought to the family.

"Everyone must have heard the noise and commotion."

Suzanne was equally furious with Uncle Jacques for chasing out her *beau garçon*. She sobbed that Eugène would never come back to such a small-town family. When Grand-mère returned she was furious with everyone, especially with Maman for talking too much.

To my mind, our scandal ended happily, for Suzanne and Eugène were married two weeks later at midnight. By that time the custom of marrying at midnight had disappeared, but Maman told my father it had to be that way. I heard her say that Monsieur Eugène had dishonored more than one family in Caen, and one of them in particular would do all they could to disrupt the ceremony should they hear of it. So at night and in secret was the way it ended, and Aunt Suzanne was happy with her soldier for a while.

At thirteen I finished school for good. In preparation for the ceremony Maman took the big step of sending me to the coiffeur. In those days people didn't wash their hair all the time, and more or less everyone had little bugs—not lice—or scales in their hair. We always talked about the bugs, the *punaises*, when

Madame Lucie's Story

I was young. One of my tricks as a child, while going over my catechism, was to call Saint Joseph not the *Père putatif* of Christ, but the *Père punaisé*. Maman always got furious with me. Anyway, the coiffeur scrubbed and scrubbed my head, which hadn't been scrubbed for months, and put it, for the last time, in long pipe curls down my back. Maman had made me a white dress, pleated all down the front, and a straw hat for the occasion. While my classmates and I sat on the stage, Monsieur le Curé presided over the ceremonies. It was boring, and I sat fidgeting and scratching my head. Maman, however, was horrified by the scene on stage, for as I scratched, my scalp began snowing all the accumulated flakes disturbed first by the coiffeur and then by my bored fingers. School for me had been one failure from beginning to end.

Yet my parents were proud of me. I was good neither at schoolwork nor in deportment; I never did my piano lessons or curtsies as well as the little *desmoiselles* with whom I went to school. My failures were visible to the citizens of Caen as, one by one, other students arose to receive their prizes in French, arithmetic, penmanship, and bearing. Suddenly Monsieur le Curé called my name. I had won the prize for needlework, which to Maman's mind—and in the opinion of many others in those days—was most important of all for young women. Papa said to everyone who congratulated me later that my skill in needlework would make me my fortune.

Instead of going on for the *brevet* like Aunt Suzanne, it was decided that I would take my apprenticeship at the age of fourteen. Maman negotiated a place for me with the Maison Herault, which was right by the courthouse and the prefecture, and which was the finest millinery establishment in the area. The great ladies like the prefect's wife, the rich lawyers' and businessmen's wives—in short, all the women of high society—went there for their hats. Far from missing school, I loved my new life of straw and lace, of crepe and feathers, even though the days were longer than I was used to. There were at least a dozen of us in the workrooms, and hats from Herault sold for twenty francs or more, whereas Maman's cost, at the most, eight or ten. Although I was young, the assistants and apprentices told me all the gossip of Caen, and I began to understand that, for all my travels around the city, a world existed that I had not seen, nor would I soon comprehend.

Once a lawyer came into the shop with a woman who was not his wife—an actress, the other girls all guessed. Within five minutes, Mme Herault's assistant Berthe was in the back room to tell us the news—how the lawyer had chosen the large pink straw hat with its swirl of tulle and ostrich feathers for his friend, how he had tickled her cheek with the feathers and then stood nervously buttoning and unbuttoning his gloves while the fancy lady primped and adjusted the hat with the help of *Madame la patronne.*

Berthe was from the outskirts of the city and was a distant cousin of the Heraults. Before she worked in hats, she had sewn for a fancy *lingère.* It was there, I guess, that she developed her eye for watching *les grands.* She kept everyone in stitches with her stories, and especially liked to repeat descriptions of trousseaus.

"For the bride Dumont we made," Berthe said, imitating the hauteur of *les grands,* "a dozen batiste and a dozen linen nightgowns—the highest quality, of course—going from chin to toes. And then we made the bridegroom two dozen more, also going from chin to toes but with a slit in front so that he could perform his duty on the wedding night." Everyone roared at the foolish ways of society people, and I did too, even though at that age I didn't understand the joke.

My apprenticeship lasted fifteen months—less than the normal time.

"You have no need for more training, Mademoiselle," the *patronne* told me, "not when you're going to work under a milliner as talented as your mother."

She was right, of course. I did have more experience than

the other apprentices who hadn't grown up with hats. I had known more about millinery when I started my apprenticeship than many knew when they finished. Still, I sensed that other factors caused the early termination of my time with Mme Herault. As the days passed, it became clear that trouble at home caused Maman to want me back.

Before life changed too drastically, however, we had our winter holidays. Noël we always celebrated with Grand-mère Levigne, the baker. Papa and the bakerboys as usual did all the cooking. We wouldn't be many that year, Aunt Suzanne having gone with Uncle Eugène to Paris to make his fortune. Nor could Uncle Jacques and his wife come because, as Maman always put it, he had just bought a new baby. So our party included only my family, Grand-mère, and my other uncle and aunt and their twins, with whom I made my famous first communion. But it was fun because Papa was always such a cut-up. He wore a chef's hat and fastened a leek to his clothing for the "order of leeks"; all great chefs belonged to some order, and Papa would be no different. Then the great chef and his helpers stuffed a turkey with chestnuts. It usually swelled so much in cooking that they had to cut it to remove the finished bird through the oven doors that were meant to receive slim loaves of bread instead of fat turkeys. But the feast was delicious. Hotel owners and restaurant chefs with whom Papa did business taught him all their cooking tricks. He became, in fact, a very good cook. Maman said that unfortunately these clients taught him about drinking too.

As we set out for Grand-mère Brun's on New Year's Day, I could tell that Maman was sad, but my father gaily drove the carriage he had rented. He sang café songs and tried to make Maman laugh the way she used to. Grand-mère Brun was also a widow, and she lived outside Caen in a small area we called the

Nouveau Monde, where the foundries have since been built. I only remember Grand-père Brun a little, always joking and poking me and my little cousins just as Papa came to do. But unlike Papa, Grand-papa Brun was huge, so huge in fact that by his bed he had installed a system of pulleys allowing him to lie down, turn, get up. Mechanical genius ran in the Brun family, so when Grandfather Brun had to retire because of his heart, Papa had no trouble stepping into the business. For as long as it flourished, we were happy.

The dining room at Grand-mère Brun's bulged with Uncle Fernand, Aunt Cécile, and their four children, with my other uncle and aunt and their two. The gardener was there, and also a strange and tiny hunchback whose wife was the most beautiful woman I had ever seen. The hunchback was one of Papa's best friends from schooldays, and it always amazed me how they kidded each other, even about the hump on the back and how Papa couldn't grow one. How the beautiful woman adored him! I loved to hear the story of her *grand amour*, which had made her insist on their marriage, even though he had not wanted to tie her down to someone so misshapen. They were the ideal in France—an inseparable couple. Each loved and protected the other with a devotion that made everyone marvel.

On New Year's Day we all ate more than we should have. Grand-mère Brun's meal for us started with a pot-au-feu and a little red wine, followed by oysters. When in good form the men put down not a dozen or two, but a hundred oysters apiece. They were, of course, the small oysters; still, all the children watched wide-eyed and counted, for this was truly amazing to us who didn't, at that age, eat everything the adults did. Then Grand-mère brought out her best Norman cider to accompany the chickens, the roast, and the rabbit.

Every time we ate rabbit at Grand-mère Brun's someone always repeated the story of Aunt Cécile's first dinner with the family. It happened to be a day when a neighbor had just presented my grandmother with a fresh hare. She had heard that my new aunt hated rabbit. In fact, in preparation for that first visit Uncle Fernand had been explicit.

"Please, Maman, serve something special—and anything but rabbit."

With a fresh hare in her kitchen and with a good sense of household economy, my grandmother forged ahead with the help of her maid, Adèle, to make it into one of their masterpieces.

"Above all," she whispered to each of us individually, "don't mention that you are eating rabbit."

Aunt Cécile was enchanted with that first dinner and, as a new bride or maybe as a dutiful daughter-in-law, wanted Grand-mère's recipe for what she thought was chicken. Then my grandmother revealed her secret to an unbelieving Cécile. Only after the rabbit's ears were presented to her would she accept that she had truly eaten what she detested most. Both my grandmothers taught me tricks and ways of dealing with foibles and problems that I never forgot.

That New Year's Day we children obediently ate the rabbit, then salad and cheese. I say obediently, but also expectantly, because we all knew that Grand-mère Brun would reward our endurance and good behavior. As she rang her little bell for the last course I could feel my skin begin to tingle and my body wriggle. Adèle's back pushed open the door. As she turned, we all gasped, while the men, led by Papa, cheered and applauded the New Year's cake—caramelized sugar and cream, candied decorations, inside all sorts of sweet fillings layered a foot high. It was passed around the table while champagne corks popped. I was about fifteen, and I thought at that moment that someday I would have my own Adèle to present me with sugared cakes at the sound of a bell. I would have champagne and a laughing gentleman who would make funny jokes and give me a New Year's embrace, as Papa was then doing to Maman.

2

World War I

Lisieux, 1910

I couldn't believe it when Maman told me we were moving away from Caen—away from regimental parades and concerts in the park, away from the bakery, theater, and circus. She had sold her boutique, and Papa was selling his business, as well as a good deal of our furniture, to settle with his creditors. He was ruined, which meant changes for all of us. I wouldn't miss things like piano lessons, but I would miss the city, our outings together, and Papa's jokes. Maman had said he wasn't coming with us.

Being an only child I was spoiled, you might say, and unprepared for life's difficulties. At school I was a rebel, at home the center of attention when there was time to give it; and even my apprenticeship had been more like an adventure allowed me by my parents. I hadn't sensed until it was over that Maman had been equipping me for what might be a difficult future. Returning home, however, it quickly became apparent that all was not well.

My mother and grandmother held councils for just the two of them. Though Maman tried to hush Grand-mère's talk whenever I came in the room, it was impossible to keep the secret from me. Grand-mère was vigorous in her belief that Maman should get a legal separation to protect her own money from my father's follies. Trying to talk softly, to hush the matter so that it might go away, Maman resisted.

"What! And cause a scandal? It would be the end of all of us—the bakery too." She was right, for in those days any kind of separation made one and all one's relatives outcasts.

The problem of Papa's follies persisted. Grand-mère's anger boiled when she thought of his wasted talent. My father was an inventive genius; his most recent project had been making surgical instruments for one of the doctors in town. But the doctor had stopped patronizing my father—too unreliable, he said. Plumbing, electricity, telephones, tools of any kind—Papa could handle all of them, and in those days, as Grand-mère never tired of pointing out, such talent was sought after.

"He might have given you a life of ease, Marie. And he's drinking the future away." My grandfather had been resilient, she continued, my father lacked character. The business had been handed to him on a silver platter; he was giving it away.

Maman tried to defend him by explaining that the expulsion of the religious orders had dealt him too heavy a blow. Ten out of twelve of the orders he serviced had migrated to Belgium. The politicians, not my father, were to blame. But her defense was weak, and she knew something had to be done. So we moved to Lisieux, Papa openly weeping as the wagonload of household goods pulled away. Maman reassured him that we wanted to see him as soon as he straightened out his affairs. At that point I was confused about just when we would be seeing him and under what conditions.

Like Caen, Lisieux was a garrison town, with soldiers quartered, it seemed, in every house. For a while we lived in a fourth-floor flat rented to us for practically nothing by a gentleman to whom Maman had explained our circumstances. Being resourceful, she quickly found a boutique with a small apartment on the floor above. Right across the way were soldiers who tried to strike up an acquaintance with both of us, for Maman was still young and beautiful.

Because of the garrison, Lisieux had the reputation in those days of being a wild city. Initially I found this improbable, for in Caen I had never been aware of the connection between soldiers and wild living. There the students had been the rowdy ones, charivariing professors who gave them bad grades, keeping girlfriends with whom they frolicked openly. They would dump buckets of water or oyster shells on the heads of comrades passing by. Maman always clucked at them, saying that this was how France made men serious. Stealing mailboxes (and almost anything else), the students at Caen were all studying to be magistrates, lawyers, and statesmen.

I didn't have time at first to give much thought to all of this, we were so busy and preoccupied. We survived until the boutique was established only because of Maman's past economies and her insistence on hard work. Instead of practicing the piano and running wild, I went to the public fountain for water, emptied chamberpots, and helped with the household chores. Life had changed a lot for me, and yet, looking around, I could see that there were many more unfortunate people.

Bad as things seemed, Maman and I did not have to work outside—in a factory, for example. For women, *that* was destitution. I watched the poor women of Lisieux coming home from work in the factory where boxes for Camembert and other Norman cheeses were made. On winter evenings they drew their capes around them against the winds and rain, their bodies pitched forward, their heads bent. On bright days, going to the fountain, I stared while they carried large baskets full of boxes. Looking back, I'm ashamed to say that once I stood laughing with the rest while one woman dropped her basket, freeing dozens of round containers to roll down the hilly streets of Lisieux.

This kind of dallying was unusual once Maman found the

boutique she wanted. We had a busy spot on the Rue Marché au Beurre between the cathedral and the nearby Carmelite convent. Now I learned what making hats was all about, and I learned the seriousness of business. After doing a frame of wire and cotton—the worst part—I would stitch yards of straw as a covering for summer hats, or for winter, velvets or wool. During periods of high activity the work would be so arduous that even my strict mother would begin to sag by ten at night. "Keep on, Lucie," she would say, "I'm going upstairs to take off my corset." She would pour a glass of wine to give us energy. When I was at the stage of decorating a hat with flowers, feathers, or bows, I didn't mind the long hours. The shapes—a napoleon, a marquise, a sailor—still were so fascinating that I couldn't envision millinery as drudgery or a desperate means of survival.

I began in those years to daydream, once in a while about a passing soldier who was particularly handsome, but mostly about Theresa of Lisieux. With her four sisters, she had been a Carmelite nun just down the hill from the boutique. Though she hadn't been canonized yet, everyone in town talked about her and the other Martin sisters. An aunt of a friend of ours had gone to school with them when they were young, and she reported that had there been ten Martin sisters each of them would have been a Carmelite, had there been twenty, then all twenty. One of them was still mother superior, but it was mostly about Theresa that everyone talked. The Little Flower, she was called, and the more the pilgrims came and the more people talked, the more certain I was that she was a saint. When a child, she had been miraculously called back from death; she had seen the Holy Virgin; and as she lay dying she said: "I will send showers of roses from Heaven to all the people on earth." She was only twenty-three when she died, on the day I was born.

So Saint Theresa occupied my thoughts a lot, and sometimes when I went for a walk I would head for the "Buissonets," the Martins' house on another hill not too far from the store. I don't remember it as being particularly grand, just inspiring, though today people report that there are roses covering the house and lovely furniture inside. I didn't go inside of course, but stalked it, you might say, and thought of what it must have been like to live there, to be a girl with long golden curls, with sisters, and a loving father.

My own daydreaming and pilgrimages were cut short as we became busier and busier. When that happened, I couldn't sew at a leisurely pace or even much of the time, for Maman had recognized my talent in selling hats. I could sell anything to anyone—a shopgirl, a country woman in for market day, or even a lady whose eye had caught sight of something in our window. I'd help them all try on a hat, praise the shape, or, if they hesitated, suggest a different bow or flower or veil.

In the off-season, we dressed dolls in marvelous clothes and put them in the window along with the hats. During those slow times we hoped to sell them to churchgoers or pilgrims or marketers. Believe me, when no one was buying hats, we were delighted to sell a doll for nine or ten francs. Maman also sewed for me in the off-season. I'll never forget the red merino dress she made me, with tiny black buttons and a red hat to match. To keep the window full, she put the hat on display until an occasion came around for me to wear it. One day when it was on display a photographer came by to take our picture—Maman, the apprentice, a little neighbor girl, and me. I scowled in the photograph, while Maman looked content. She had just sold my red hat to a grand lady for her daughter.

We made friends among the tradespeople of Lisieux. The son of Charles Lemaître, who wrote songs in patois, was a coiffeur on the corner, and Mme Blanc ran a saddlery just across the street. Mme Norman, who ran the château of the Sadi-Carnot family, became particularly close. She told us about the great family for whom she worked: Mme Sadi-Carnot—his second wife—was from Lisieux, and a street was named after her. As we began to fit in, the city seemed almost as good as Caen. And when Papa joined us, life was gay again.

Perhaps it wasn't so gay for Papa; he had to work for other people now, but with his talent those who employed him called him their right-hand man. One plumbing establishment sent him to the Carmelite convent regularly. He even talked to the mother superior, the sister of the Little Flower, Theresa. I pumped him for every detail of life at the convent—Mother Agnes' heavy veil, the bell he rang to warn the other nuns he was in their area. Once he brought back a special message to me from one of the Martin sisters.

While we were in Lisieux the mayor began allowing religious processions again. According to Maman, he was an anti-clerical, but his wife and daughter were devout. I imagined his daughter pleading with him to protect the saints and sacrament, but Maman said the mayor knew how good the Church was for business. The pilgrims to Sister Theresa's grave helped the hotels and restaurants and the printers who made cards and booklets.

During this time the Carmelites held a great ceremony to move Theresa's remains within the convent church. Horses, fine costumes, refreshments, altars along the route of the procession—the *commerçants* of Lisieux provided them all. We were always busy at those times making gladiola crowns for the wealthy girls—the children of Mary, they were called—who accompanied it, and new hats for their mothers.

Funerals and death also kept us occupied, and we always hoped they would come in the off-season. Death meant having hats ready the next day, or in two days at the very latest. Sometimes we sewed all night attaching long veils bordered with black crepe to the hats. For good customers we would adjust old mourning clothes to fit or to make them more fashionable. Unfortunately, the morning after an all-night session the store had to open at eight as usual, and all the regular chores faced us as well.

I was the one who put the household waste on the street to be taken to the fertilizer merchants, went to get water, then tended the store if Maman had to shop or go off to do the laundry. This she did in the Touques River running behind the hotel—the same river in which the hotel dumped its waste. The sewing was more urgent than in Caen. When we had to do the chores in these conditions, I knew life had changed. Caen was clean, with indoor plumbing and public garbage cans called Perrotines after the mayor who thought of them—just like the Poubelles of Paris. Lisieux lacked such comforts and cleanliness, and there I slowly grew aware of what life could have in store.

I was seventeen in 1913, and since moving Maman had watched me with eyes that seemed to be everywhere. Lisieux being a garrison town, soldiers were quartered all around us, and café life was loud and sometimes rowdy. A customer of our boutique, in return for a blessing Sister Theresa sent her from heaven, bought one of the worst cafés near us and turned it into a store for religious medals and books. Sometimes the city seemed but a battleground for the extremely religious and the soldiers. But what Maman called the "bad morals" of the city made her strict where I was concerned. She began giving me an exact amount of time for fetching water or running an errand. She allowed me to talk only with our neighboring tradespeople, especially Mme Blanc at the saddlery. That was the limit of my solitary adventures; at seventeen I was almost under house arrest and it rankled because Caen had been such a different story.

In the season, Maman, Papa, and I still went to Trouville to watch the boardwalk strollers, whose manners and costumes captivated me more than ever. Later I realized that the best in Parisian fashion, the highest of French society had passed before me, all on that single boardwalk of my youth. We also took picnics to the country, where our favorite place was a tiny hostel named Le Chien. The owners provided salad, cheese, and a drink, but Maman always brought our own Camembert—theirs was too dry, she said—and a bottle from our supply of cider. People in Normandy always preferred choosing their own Camembert or Livarot, or drinking cider made by the presses that stopped at each house after the harvest. I understood these ways, but not the practice of imprisoning young girls.

Yet, right under Maman's eyes, I met soldiers. They talked to me while I brought our waste to the doorstop. In those days, it was natural to say a little *bonjour* to one's neighbor while holding a chamber pot, whose contents would soon be fertilizing Norman fields. As I opened the shutters or watered the flowers in the windowboxes, a passing soldier might stop for a second, and I was polite. Often the young men quartered on the second floor of the house facing ours waved to me. How could one avoid soldiers in a city like this?

On my excursions to fetch water, I tried to see as much as I could, especially the pilgrims, and also the goods in shop windows. One day, rather preoccupied with the sights and with the water jar, I saw two soldiers approaching. Not alert enough to the situation, we met at a point where the sidewalk was narrow, bounded by a building on one side and a horsehitch on the other. The first soldier leaned politely toward the building while I navigated past the horsehitch, my water jar not making things easier. Suddenly we were bottlenecked, for my skirt had caught in the hitch. I remained its prisoner, spilling water in my effort to move, until the soldier released me. The soldier was Philippe, friend of the young men across the street. Later, he said he had vowed to marry me at that very moment he saw me blushing and discomfited by our unexpected brush together.

From that time on Philippe passed by our boutique whenever possible, and I arranged to be at the counter, or even better, out watering the plants when I thought he might be passing. I looked for him and thought of him almost continually. Maman did not help matters any by singing her romantic songs, like the

"Polka à Moustache," while we worked. I knew it was wrong to be thinking of soldiers, to meet a beau in this way, but there was no help for me. After weeks of this, one day I came into the store, having talked to Philippe while I (slowly, very slowly) closed the shutters.

"Who was that young man with you out there?" Maman asked sternly.

"Just a passing soldier, Maman," I replied.

"Enough of these stories. You are not to leave this building, and above all you are not to talk to that soldier again."

There was nothing to say. One didn't argue with parents in those days. But that evening I wrote a note to Philippe explaining our problem. Next morning, the apprentice, sent to do my usual errands, took the note to a café where Philippe had told me he could be found in emergencies. She returned and, when Maman left the workroom, reported that he had indeed been in the café but had said nothing after reading the note.

My heart began to break. A dream of Philippe had taken over my life, and I couldn't accept that this, too, would have to end. I was sitting, desperate at the possibility, when a letter arrived for my parents. Maman took a long time reading it, then tucked it away. When Papa came home she handed it to him. Somehow I knew it was from Philippe, so much had Maman looked at me that day. Finally, they told me that he might visit me at home. Philippe had explained himself so finely that Maman called him "honorable."

In those visits, while we all sat and talked together, Philippe won my parents over, and before I knew it we were engaged to be married. What a time! How improbable! Philippe was an orphan, a soldier, a stranger to all of us. Yet we were going to get married. Maman and I started sewing, and the first thing we made was a new dress and hat for me to wear on an engagement trip to my grandmother's in Caen. Philippe wore his best uniform and met us at the train station with a white bouquet and a tiny ring for me. I have never been so happy and will always remember the day—July 14, the *fête nationale*, 1914. Three weeks later Philippe went off to war.

I did something unusual for our family by writing letters every day for three months until, in October, Philippe was killed. Some time later we held a family reunion and had our picture taken: Papa and his brother with their joking smiles; Maman in mourning out of respect and love for my fiancé; I, in mourning also, having vowed never to marry.

The death of Philippe made this war the most important and least significant event of my life. That moment—his death—lasted forever; and then nothing else about wartime touched me. Besides, compared to the regions north and east of us we hardly suffered. Battles weren't fought on our fields; we weren't occupied; neither combatants nor wounded, nor ambulances nor munitions crossed our paths. Maman and I continued making hats, but our ingenuity was tested as luxury fabrics became scarce. We sewed with felt instead of silk, and especially we made mourning hats until, after a couple of years, every woman in Lisieux and the countryside had one. So you can see that while many people would thereafter be obsessed by the story of the war, for me it would always and only mean the death of Philippe.

I avoided the glances of soldiers now, though the city was packed with them. Though most people favored Bernadette of Lourdes, Saint Theresa occupied my thoughts more than ever, and Maman, with her hardheadedness and practical sense, thought me a little crazy. Papa, however, brought me stories of the Carmelite convent, and even a word of comfort and blessing, so he said, from the mother superior herself.

But I was young, and one day in 1916 I met another soldier, with whom, as the expression goes, I fell in love at first sight. Entering our boutique to find corporal's stripes, Pierre was handsome in his uniform and his curled moustache. He was also a dozen years older than I. But here is the ridiculous part. He was staying in Lisieux only three days, he wrote in warning from a café after our first meeting. He had seen his brother killed at his side, had suffered so great a shock from it that the military had judged him unfit for further combat duty. Our little friendship would probably end, he said, because the next day he would be guarding German prisoners in Caen. While reading the letter, I had grown sad all over again. Finally the word *Caen* registered. Surely, I thought, there must be a way back to my native city.

Soon after, I was having a little talk with Mme Blanc in her saddlery, when that good lady mentioned some business she had to do in Caen.

"Oh, do let me go with you, Madame, " I suggested, "and your trip will be so much easier."

So much was she against the idea that I had to reveal my situation. Instead of finding me silly, Mme Blanc sympathized. I had suffered enough, she decided, to deserve a little diversion. War had changed many people's minds about behavior, or at least it had softened them. Maybe the trip would take my mind off the past and change my gloomy outlook.

That afternoon, Mme Blanc came bustling into our boutique and put the proposal to Maman without revealing that it had been my idea.

"You don't want to be burdened with an extra responsibility," Maman commented, shaking her head.

"To the contrary, Madame, little Mlle Lucie will be a big help to me with her knowledge of the city. I have much to do in Caen and no time to waste getting lost."

Within two days we were off to Caen in the same little train that I had ridden with Philippe. Only I didn't think of him. Instead I plotted how I would tell the guard on duty that I was Pierre's sister, and while scheming I had to keep up a conversation with Mme Blanc, who felt it her duty to fill me with cautionary remarks.

We stepped off the train and headed for the garrison headquarters, through the streets where I had played at diabolo, where I had chased with my friends after adventure. That day I felt Maman's grim determination prodding me along, but I also knew that Papa's sense of play would have to inspire my words.

The soldier on duty politely asked me my business, and I told him more politely that I wanted to see soldier Leclerc.

"But there is no soldier Leclerc at Caen," he replied.

"Oh yes, certainly there is," I replied, "he came from Lisieux several days ago to guard prisoners."

"Well, suppose he is here? What is your business with him?"

"I am his sister and he has sent for me." There it was, and in telling the lie, I looked earnest and sisterly.

"You want me to believe, Mademoiselle, that you are the sister of soldier Lemaire, guard of German prisoners, and you do not know his name?"

It was true. I stumbled over the name that I had heard but once and to my humiliation now had imperfectly remembered.

I started to make a joke, as Papa would have done, but before it was out, an older soldier, whom I think I knew from childhood, appeared.

"Why Mlle Brun! What brings you back to Caen and how are your mother and father?" My humiliation deepened as I tried to make my story as respectable as possible.

"Well, Mademoiselle, I'll go tell Lemaire you are here to bring him a personal welcome to Normandy from the citizens of Caen and Lisieux."

As the soldier turned toward the barracks, another fear passed through my mind. What if Pierre had forgotten who I was and refused to come? What, even worse, if he appeared and joined in the general ridicule of my position? Even darker thoughts started surfacing, but at that moment Pierre came forward quickly and shook my hand with sincere pleasure. My old soldier friend arranged a few hours off-duty for him on that day and for my successive visits to Caen. The good Mme Blanc suddenly had much business in that city every ten days or so, and, as she told Maman, I had become indispensable to her success.

At that time I thought Maman didn't know my secret, but it seems impossible that Mme Blanc at some point hadn't told her. In any case she didn't miss me, as there was hardly any work at the store, business was so bad in 1917. One day I suggested finding some other occupation, some other way of supplementing our falling income. Maman was shocked by the suggestion, but Mme Norman, visiting town that day from the Sadi-Carnot estate, immediately picked up the theme.

"You know, Madame, your little Lucie has good ideas. And I know where she might help most. The regimental headquarters just a few streets over is looking for a young woman to do its paperwork. I'll go with her to inquire about a position."

Maman never refused recommendations from successful women like Mme Norman or Mme Blanc. Before I knew it, I was in the medical corps with several other girls my age. Our office had charge of provisioning troops in the area, and the operation was managed by big businessmen who had now become colonels and captains for the war effort. They joked with us, taught us how to forge their signatures on requisitions: "Give me a fancy 'Dubois,' " Colonel Dubois would say, and I'd attempt his name with garlands of curlicues. How different it was from working with Maman, with all these very important men around. Each was separated from his family, and I soon discovered that each had his *petite amie* chosen from my fellow workers.

Soon after I began with the Service de Santé, Mme Blanc did her last good deed on my behalf. She bustled again into the store one Sunday and told Maman that a friend of a friend of her family was stationed in Caen guarding German prisoners.

"I've seen the young man several times, Madame, and he would be perfect for Lucie."

Now to Maman's way of thinking this was the proper way of arranging couples. I listened without showing interest, but aware that with my new work, Mme Blanc was again solving the problem of seeing Pierre. Even at that, even should Maman agree, there was one final barrier that only Pierre and I knew.

"You are very nice, Mme Blanc," Maman replied, "but we've had enough of soldiers in wartime. Things are much too uncertain."

"Just let him pay his respects with me next Sunday, and let us see. It will be a nice diversion for all of us."

Maman couldn't resist, the way she might have in her confident young womanhood. Business was precarious, both my grandmothers were now dead, and Maman had developed a cough that annoyed her. When Pierre visited that Sunday she was too weak not to be charmed, and Papa, of course, loved people.

At the end of the visit Papa suggested that Pierre visit the next week. Before long we went walking together arm in arm, Pierre holding me close to his side. Soon, he thought, we should become engaged. I was twenty-one now, and he was almost ten years older. We had only one problem: Pierre was married.

At any other time, I wouldn't have thought of looking at a married man, but war was different. Besides, being spoiled and headstrong, I felt that I should have the person I loved no matter what. From the first Pierre had explained his situation. Before the war he had worked for the Pathé brothers, our great film makers. He had set up their theaters around France, and while doing this work in Nancy had met a woman with whom he eloped. But war came, and when he went home on his first leave, his wife had left without a trace. Pierre was now in the process of getting a divorce, and even though it was not his fault, as one would say, still the whole business was scandalous.

My parents were astonished when we finally told them. Maman looked grim, even though Pierre was so obviously upset at having to talk of his own humiliation over the divorce procedure. Seeing my determination, Papa did nothing more than give his assent, but after Pierre left, he fumed.

"Oh, it's unfortunate to have an only daughter, and her about to marry a divorced man."

In spite of everything I was happy. My job gave me some diversion; Pierre visited on weekends; and in spare moments Maman and I sewed on my trousseau. One of our suppliers brought enough fine linen for a dozen sheets, while Maman found a second-grade fabric for twelve more. The stitching brought us together on a happy project, and it seemed to me that my mother was sharing my joy to some extent. Then, right in the middle of it all, the war took Pierre to Salonika on the Balkan front—even though he was unfit, so the army decreed, for active service. Before leaving, in those last sad moments, he asked that I stop working for the Service de Santé.

By this time, though not proud of working, I had come to take it as a matter of course, and the money helped us all.

"I know that, *chérie*," he said, "but I also know what goes on in those offices. Unprotected women shouldn't be working, and besides, you'll have enough to do getting ready for marriage."

That made me smile and agree. I was glad that Pierre saw himself as my protector. He was also many other things. From Salonika he sent wonderful drawings and cards to my parents, letters to me full of reassurance. I was frightened at what might happen to him and I was frightened at what was going on around us. Influenza raged through all of France, hitting our neighbors, even killing them—the butcher's wife a few doors away, some of our past customers, and Mme Norman's husband on leave from the war. What a blow that was! The Normans knew everyone in both city and countryside, taking the place of the grand seigneurs, who were occupied by the Parisian social life. Hundreds of people appeared for the funeral, and afterward Mme Norman provided dinner for more than 250 of them, including Papa.

Suddenly the war ended, and my fiancé was on his way

home. I was never patient, so the wait was unbearable—and I was, too. Mme Blanc came to the rescue for the last time by taking me off on a trip to Paris. Maman gathered enough material to make me a new hat, besides those she had prepared for my trousseau. Even though I had never traveled much—one didn't in those days—I didn't expect to look like a peasant. Yet Trouville days, when I had seen society people and fashions, were far behind, so I worried. We arrived at the crowded Gare St. Lazare and were walking past the Printemps store, when whom should I meet but one of my father's sisters, who designed clothing for high-society women. Life is full of such coincidences, though I thought nothing much about that on this first visit to Paris. My head was too full of marriage plans for Mme Blanc's cure to have any effect.

Pierre returned, and together we waited for his divorce to be settled. Meanwhile, news of my impending marriage traveled the neighborhood, though we tried to keep it secret because of the circumstances. Our priest stopped me one day to offer his congratulations.

"This will be a fine marriage for the parish, Mlle Brun."

"I'm afraid not, Father. My fiancé is divorced." I explained the desertion by Pierre's wife, but that didn't soften his stern look.

"Well, Mademoiselle, I'm going to have to excommunicate you. Come back after the wedding and we'll see what it takes to straighten things out. I'll be waiting for you."

With that he turned back to the church, probably to start filling the forms and counting the costs for my reinstatement. I can assure you, he's still waiting for me.

We were married July 22, 1919, in a small and quiet ceremony because of this new scandal. My uncles and aunts all came, and our neighbors, the merchants, lodged all of them except for Uncle Jacques, who very grandly stayed in a hotel. Everyone was good to us—Mme Norman sent in five chickens, five rabbits, five liters of cream, five kilos of butter, and five bottles of calvados for our feasting. Still my parents' nerves were agitated because we couldn't be married in church. They wondered how it would affect Papa's work for the convent. But when we woke up the day of the wedding it was pouring as if it had never rained before, so instead of a procession through town to the Hôtel de Ville, we took carriages, without being observed.

For three days the family celebrated. Pierre, now my excellent husband, and I spent our wedding night at my parents'. It was a shock, I can tell you, because except for my few months as an apprentice, I had never heard much about sex.

But we had good customs in Normandy. People sang all the time in those days. Celebrating a holiday or walking arm in arm through the countryside, we'd sing "Les Noctambules" or "Le Petit Tonkinois." Like a good Norman, I've always loved singing.

In any case, that night after my husband and I had gone to our room, after things began to seem strange to me, suddenly clanging and singing broke out, my father's voice louder than all the rest:

> Said the mattress to the sheets
> I have never seen such feats.
> Said the pillow to the case
> We've been shaken to the base.

Pierre and I giggled, holding one another until we went to sleep.

On July 25 I left Normandy to begin a new life with my handsome soldier husband. We had trunks of linens and housewares. My parents had given me several sets of silver dishes and utensils, and two precious silver goblets. I had clothes, it seemed, to last forever, but nothing so beautiful as the pigeon-

gray suit and rose-colored hat Maman had made. We said
good-by to all our relations, then to Maman and Papa, sadly, at
the train station, for we were off to Paris to see Pierre's parents.
They wouldn't receive me in their home, so we would meet at
the train station. But I had no fear any more, even though they
didn't approve of their son's divorce and remarriage. Then we
would change trains for Marseille, where Pierre had an important job disposing of war inventories. I had always wanted to see
the world, even when I was four, and now I had someone to do
it with. On the train, in the midst of our happiness, I taught
Pierre one more Norman song:

> Debout enfants de Normandie
> Devant un passé glorieux.
> Le regard franc. L'âme hardie.
> Voilà comme étaient nos aïeux,
> Dominateurs et rois de l'onde
> A travers les flots écumants.
> Ils ont jusqu'au confins du monde
> Promener le drapeau normand.
> C'est un normand, m'a dit ma mère,
> C'est un normand qu'a conquis l'Angleterre.

> [Arise all ye of Normandy
> To praise our glorious past.
> Fierce of eye and strong of heart,
> Our fathers long held fast
> Dominion of the Northern sea.
> Then on the shore they cast
> Their die, and over many lands
> They raised their Norman flag at last.
> > It was a Norman, Mother said to me,
> > A Norman conquered England o'er the sea.]

3

Between the Wars

Miramas, 1919

Southern France seemed poor by comparison to the fat richness of my native Normandy—no trees heavy with fruit, no abundance of cream, butter, and Camembert. I saw only scrub, not hedgerows and grassy pastures, heard only the mistral, which fulfilled its promise of making one grumpy or even crazy, and watched boys tend scraggly sheep. But the people were like jewels I had sometimes seen on Parisiennes at Trouville. They sparkled, welcoming me more warmly than the finest Norman, even though they disliked my cold northern accent.

We took a small house in Miramas, just a few fields away from the depot for war supplies. Pierre worked at taking inventory and disposing of the strange goods that the Americans had sent—cans by the thousands of corned beef, typewriter ribbons, and I can't tell you everything else. But I formed my first idea of what Americans were like by the enormous quantities and the exotic nature of what they sent—not a dozen but a million bottles of green ink. Pierre was foreman, I guess you would call it, of a large group of men discharging these things. While he worked, I tried to keep a good Norman house, with coffee always ready for my neighbors in this tiny place where friendliness was a way of life.

And I tried to be a good wife. For our first meal in Miramas, I made Pierre soup—he loved soup—and a chop with a custard for dessert. He praised everything.

"But is there any more?" he asked. I realized at once that the soup I had worked so hard at and the chop were seamstresses' food, hardly enough for an active young man. Had we been in Caen, I could have taken a big enamel bowl next door to the charcuterie and gotten more soup with two scoops of cream, or a big plate of white beans with cream as well.

"Don't worry, *ma poule*," He said nicely, "I'll just cook some macaroni." And he did. But despite my husband's goodness, from that moment on I always worried about having enough food or finding things that were edible. Southerners used olive oil for all their cooking—even for frying eggs—and it was almost impossible to find butter. But I searched all the more, because the thought of eggs cooked in oil turned my stomach.

Soon after we arrived and in the midst of this homesickness for Norman ways, Pierre came home with an announcement that the next day we would make a trip to Marseille. Here was the adventure I had been waiting for, so I made ready my pigeon-gray suit and rose-colored hat. I felt like a child again in search of Queen Navalo, as we walked through the narrow streets of this cosmopolitan city. There were Arabs all covered over with yards of cloth from head to toe, and blacks from the colonies in strange mixtures of colors. Men were hired on here without working papers, so at the harbor, sailors of every nationality yelled in languages I had never heard. Even the French ones used strange expressions in strange accents. In doorways and windows of certain streets women stood practically naked. For the first time, what Maman had said about Aunt Suzanne—that she knew the world too well—was beginning to make some sense.

From that trip to Marseille I date my coming of age. My

routine in Miramas remained the same, but the routine had new colors, And then, also, things happened that made me feel no longer a child. Some evenings Pierre invited soldiers who helped him at work over to play cards or talk in the evenings. I sat and sewed while they talked about politics or the big bosses or elections. It reminded me of Papa and his men's talk I sometimes heard. When it was election day he would put on his best suit, polish his shoes, and Maman would coach him.

"Why don't you take Lucie with you?" she would suggest. "You know how she loves an outing." And it was certainly true. But Papa would always refuse with a little speech about the seriousness of elections.

"The polling place shouldn't be cluttered up with crowds of chattering women and children."

So I listened to the young men as my mother might have done had she not been always working on her own business. Sometimes they talked to me about their families or made a little joke. Paul LeGoff, who lived with his mother nearby, paid particular attention to me, and I knew that Pierre was disturbed by it. Having many a time shown LeGoff the door, at long last, he said that Paul LeGoff was wild, lazy, and drank too much.

"I don't want him near this house again. He makes trouble everywhere he goes."

I didn't understand my husband's warning until several weeks later, when Pierre arrived home at noon with the news that LeGoff had been arrested the night before for killing someone playing cards in a café. Almost before the words were out of his mouth, Mme LeGoff was at our door pleading with Pierre to do something for her son. My good husband did go to the jail and then to see some officials. There was nothing to be done, and eventually Paul LeGoff was guillotined. I remember being out shopping and seeing him in custody. We said *bonjour* to each other—he had never done anything bad to me—and then I never saw him again.

Madame Lucie's Story

I wrote all this news to Maman, who responded by asking for more and by advising me on how to conduct myself.

"You are blessed with a good husband, my daughter." I remember the letters well. "Learn to make him happy, and especially work on your cooking."

That suggestion I took, and with the further help of my neighbors became an expert in making *boeuf à la mode*. I would take a kilo of carrots and some stew meat, garlic, and onions—though never so much garlic as my friends there suggested—and let them cook for hours. How good it tasted!

Maman sent other news. She and Papa missed me, even though Papa was busier than ever working for the owner of Le Petit Normand cheese factory. How silly, she wrote next, to be separated from one's only child. She thought that a nice trip to the south would help her cough, which was getting worse. Finally, in December, I received a letter from my mother saying that she had sold the boutique and that Papa had told the owner of Le Petit Normand that they were moving to Miramas.

"He had tears in his eyes when your father left," Maman reported. And I was glad that my father had finally been appreciated.

They arrived in time for Noël, and with my husband's approval. With five rooms in our house, we could all fit without too much trouble. And, to tell the truth, it would be nice to have my parents' company during the day while Pierre was gone.

The visit started badly. Pierre and I waited at the station, and when the train stopped we found each other quickly, with embraces all around. My parents went to claim their trunks, only to find them missing. Pierre went for several days to the railroad office to trace their belongings. After several weeks it became clear that my parents had truly lost everything and would live from now on from what they had in two suitcases. But we had other things to think about, for by that winter I was clearly pregnant.

Maman and I had our work cut out for us. We started knitting and sewing until we had enough clothes for the baby's first year. I bought fabric for diapers and made four dozen. Even before the delivery, I saw how to take care of them. Several neighbor women with children took their diapers, which they had already boiled, to the fields and spread them out to bleach in the sun. Then they walked around with a watering can sprinkling the diapers with a fine spray. By the end of the process each one took home a huge stack smelling fresh like the meadows.

I bought a wicker cradle—a "Moses" it was called after the basket in which Miriam had placed her tiny brother—and made coverings of muslin and white tulle. Maman made roses from scraps of silk. Truly, the "Moses" looked like a little angel's bed. The midwife came to call and had some coffee. The end of August, she said, would see my baby arrive. All the preparations cheered my parents up. Not only did they feel homesick, but Maman seemed to be coughing more and growing weaker every day.

Not all the sewing, not the midwife—nothing prepared me for what happened that August. I began my labor with some twinges of a kind I had had on and off during my pregnancy, and then the water broke. When that happened the midwife stopped in and put me to bed, where my mind wandered in between the pain.

For the first time, I started thinking about the baby. Were it a girl, I wanted her to be like Theresa of the Carmelites, with long blond curls. Sometimes on Sundays in Lisieux Papa had released me from my house arrest, and together we walked up to "Les Buissonets," tall and made of brick, a place for *les grands*. Yet Theresa, I felt then, was plain and pure despite her possessions. So I wanted a girl.

After the first day of labor my husband took time off from his job to stay with me. The midwife had given me a sheet—I guess it was to clench for the pain—and I clenched while she put cool compresses of vinegar solution on my forehead. Pierre tried to relieve things by talking about our courtship. He remembered the time we had gone to a carnival together and I had won a goose. Not wanting to cook it, Maman had commissioned a restaurant to prepare our trophy. But the goose refused at the last moment and headed out into the city, which had just been hit by a summer rainstorm. Out we went after him—Pierre, the cook, and I—getting soaked, but getting, finally, the goose.

My husband was good through it all. On the third day, I began screaming with the pain. He tore his own shirt for me to clench instead of the coarse sheet. Occasionally Pierre would leave to talk to my mother, who was too weak to climb the stairs to see me. Just a few weeks before labor started, I had learned that she was dying. We had been on a picnic—the four of us—and I had a huge appetite, while Maman ate practically nothing. She had taken a few bites of her sausage, then offered it to me.

"Here, Lucie," she said. "Give that baby some more food. I've had plenty."

Before I could take Maman's plate, Pierre reached for it and ate the sausage himself.

"Lucie doesn't need any more. By the looks of her, that baby's so big, he'll be lucky to get out."

At that moment Pierre didn't know the truth in what he was saying, but he did know something else. That night when we were in bed he told me.

"Don't ever, for your sake and the sake of the child, take anything to eat that your mother has touched."

I should not have pressed him for a reason, but I was so insistent that he told me the doctor had diagnosed Maman's sickness as tuberculosis. He was certain, though he had told only Pierre, that she wouldn't last a year. I cried all night and stayed in bed the next morning, while Pierre told my parents that, for all the southern sunshine, I had caught a Norman-style cold.

Two hours in the birth canal—that's how long the baby stayed. Fortunately, a baby's head is divided in four parts so that it can make the passage. I no longer knew what was happening; the pain was so constant it seemed like being dead.

But then he was born. I guess I had fainted, because suddenly the noise of the hot room hit me. The midwife was cooing, but also rubbing the baby with rum to make him cry. Finally he started making little squeaks, and then a squalling sound came out of him. Pierre was like a soldier through it all. He alternately removed bloody sheets—fourteen of them in all—looked at his new son, and tried to make me comfortable. As I think back, I imagine that he had seen worse in the war.

We sent a telegram to Pierre's parents in Paris, and we gave the baby a name. The midwife reminded us of this last task, for the baby's birth had to be registered. After just a little discussion, Pierre agreed to my wish that the baby be named after my dead fiancé, Philippe.

"That's a good choice," the midwife commented, for she knew the whole story. "Monsieur is a saint toward his wife. And now I must be off and leave this new family to get acquainted."

Pierre started to settle the bill, but the midwife refused.

"Madame has suffered too much, so this will be a baby paid for in friendship. Besides, I'll probably be back in a year, and you can pay me for the next one."

Pierre took her downstairs and then returned. He looked at me sternly.

"No more babies after this, and especially none next year."

Then he picked up little Philippe from his "Moses" and showed him to me. I was too weak to do more than sob at looking at him—he was so ugly. A misshapen head, a flattened nose, eyes not level because his head was grotesque—that was the baby I had imagined would be golden-haired and beautiful like Saint Theresa. However plump and robust he otherwise seemed—and I had felt for myself all eight pounds of him—I cried for several days about his temporary deformation. And my mother, whom Pierre carried upstairs to have her first look, didn't make me feel better.

"What an ugly child," was her only remark. And then she turned her attention to me.

I stayed in bed for almost a month and tried to nurse the baby myself as Maman had done for me. But it didn't work and I couldn't understand why. I'm very full-breasted, and I just couldn't do it, even following the midwife's instruction. So we switched to baby bottles and put a little drop of calvados in each—our Norman custom—to keep the baby from getting worms. Meanwhile, for about two weeks each neighbor woman made a visit, carrying with her the customary offering—bread, an egg, and a box of matches:

> Plein comme un oeuf
> Blanc comme le pain
> Droit comme des broquettes
>
> [Chockful as an egg
> White as bread
> Straight as matches]

After the month of convalescing, I returned to normal life, only now as a mother and a wife. What a change in less than a year and a half! My first duty was being churched. So alone I set off and offered my prayers to Saint Anne for having committed the sin of fleshly contact. We also christened Philippe. Papa was godfather and Maman the godmother, but the midwife had to take her place because she was too weak. During the service all the children congregated outside, and as we began to leave, we could hear them chanting in patois:

> If the godparents put nothing in our sack,
> May the child grow up with a bad hunchback.

We gave them something, but whether it was candy or money, I forget.

Fortunately little Philippe, after our first bad time together, was a quite handsome, model child. He began laughing, especially when Papa played with him. I enjoyed him, enjoyed taking care of his little things, but events moved and changed too fast for that enjoyment to last.

By Christmas Maman was clearly dying. After the New Year 1921 I wrote to Aunt Suzanne of what was happening. She lived in Paris now, where Uncle Eugène had in fact made his fortune. Every year they sent pictures of themselves and their three beautiful children. They looked so prosperous and handsome—the boy in his sailor suit, the two girls in lacy organdy dresses, their hair all set in long pipe curls. How far away my childhood was! By the time Aunt Suzanne telegraphed to say that she would be arriving, Maman was dead—forty-seven years old. My aunt for once proved her worth by taking charge of everything and by arranging for Maman to be buried in the cemetery of Père Lachaise, where only people with Parisian contacts may rest. And no more can I say about my dear mother's death except that such an event changes one's ideas and begins to give one character.

Soon after, I realized that Philippe would not be an only child, in spite of our agreeing not to have any more children. Before there was time to reflect on that, Papa, too, was dying. When the doctor in the area said he could do nothing, I wrote again to Aunt Suzanne, and she called us to Paris. Papa and I went and registered him in a hospital, where they diagnosed cancer of the throat. By July he was dead and buried, far from me but next to Maman in Père Lachaise. From that moment I began hating and having depressions in months that began with J.

The midwife had been right. A few days after Philippe's first birthday, she came again to deliver another baby—a boy we named Antoine. He only weighed a bit under four pounds, but he was beautiful—tiny little fingers the size of matches, a perfectly shaped head and features. The baby being so tiny, my labor lasted under two hours. I've always said that little Antoine had taken more trouble to get in than he did to get out.

One weekend soon after, when the babies were both napping, my husband and I were taking a walk in the fields around Miramas. Even after two and a half years of marriage and six of taking walks together, he loved to link his arm in mine and draw me close to his side. Although seasons don't make as much difference in the south as in Normandy, I sensed a difference, now that September was almost over—but maybe it was my Norman imagination. Suddenly we saw a constable rushing toward us and waving his arms. He was shouting about fire, and my mind flashed to the babies. But quickly his message came through that the American supply depot was on fire. Pierre set out after him.

That night Pierre returned with the news that everything was destroyed, including, he said, his job in a few days. In a certain sense, besides the job, we had lived from the supply yard's corned beef and hams. Even though they might have maggots crawling on the surface, it was stupid to throw food away. Still, we were better off than most people. Though the war and my father's illness had taken a good deal of his money, we had enough to keep us going for a while, but not forever. Pierre set off looking for work, and after some months he found a position at the Kuhlmann chemical plant near Port-de-Bouc.

We moved with everything packed in a wagon Pierre had hired. He had found us another house slightly away from the working section of town. Behind this house was a shed, which suddenly was full of possibilities. Because Pierre had started as an unskilled worker at Kuhlmann, we wouldn't have much to live on. We decided to fix up the shed and rent it out to Kuhlmann workers. My sewing life returned as I made curtains and coverlets for two beds. I bought oilcloth to cover a small table we had left over from the large house in Miramas. And two tenants quickly materialized, both of them from the colonies, an Algerian and a black man.

We were close to the sea now, where I watched President Millerand inaugurate the revolving bridge at Martigues and saw the *Prince Napoleon* launched. At the launching all the shipbuilders cried; for them it meant the end of steady work. I took the little boys on outings, but not too many. Always on edge, I worried about the Kuhlmann plant. The more responsibility Pierre acquired in the sulfate division, the more accidents and even tragedies seemed to occur: fires, small explosions, burns and wounds from the chemicals. In minutes one worker was even "eaten alive," so to speak, when he fell into a vat of corrosives. Mostly I felt uneasy being away from any neighbors, any family, any people in general. How hard it was for a shopkeeper's daughter to live an isolated life!

One night Pierre was called out to fix a machine at the plant, and I was terrified. I sat in with the sleeping children to give myself some sort of company, but my mind kept creating horrible scenes of violence. In the midst of my nightmarish thoughts, pounding began at the doors and windows. At first I decided to crawl behind Philippe's bed, then to look out the window to confront my fate.

"Who are you? What do you want?"

The pounding stopped, and in front of the glass appeared first the face of my black tenant and then of the Algerian.

"We see Monsieur Lemaire. He say take care of you, Miss. We just want to say, we take care of you. Don't be afraid." And they vanished.

Things change. That is what life has taught me. By the beginning of spring 1923 we were destitute. Pierre, though he had quickly become a foreman at Kuhlmann, was just as quickly out of a job, along with a lot of other men. We lived on the little money left from my parents and tried to decide what to do.

Madame Lucie's Story

When we had only one case of condensed milk for the children and one case of canned herring left for us, we had hit what seemed the bottom. There was only one thing to do, and we did it. I took some jewelry of Maman's, sold it, and we headed for Paris and Pierre's parents.

Neither of us was thrilled with the idea. Pierre knew there were problems going back, particularly because his parents had not approved of his divorce and remarriage. They hadn't come to our wedding, and that upset him. I was unhappy about the shame of it all, of going like beggars to be taken in by someone else, and especially by people who were so different from my own. Then there was the additional problem that these people hadn't wanted Pierre to marry me and hadn't received me at first. But they took us in.

Pierre's mother was a strong woman who had raised six sons. She had also had a daughter who died very young. Olga was her name, and I remember Maman telling me that I had almost been named Olga, so great was the rage for Russian names from the start of our alliance with that country in the 1890s. If you think of it, many French words come from Russian, like *bistro*, which has something to do with quickness. Olga must have been born about the same time I was.

The sons were another story again. Pierre's mother always complained that all she had had to do was sit down to mend her husband's underwear and she would be pregnant. One day, when she was feeling ill from what she thought was the onset of menopause, the doctor came and gave her an examination.

"How many children do you have, Madame?" he asked.

"Six," she replied, for Olga was still alive.

"Well, soon you will have seven." She was pregnant again with the last boy.

I could tell from her goodness to all of us that she was a fine mother. Her sons for the most part found steady work in the automobile and electric plants around Courbevoie, and one of her granddaughters became a professor at the Sorbonne.

Pierre's father could joke too, and he joked like Papa with
me after we became acquainted. Someone would drop in for a
visit, calling from the garden gate. My father-in-law would
greet the newcomer.

"Come meet my daughter-in-law who's staying with us.
She's a real Norman, as you can see from her basket full of
chickens, rabbits, butter, and cream." How he reminded me of
Papa!

But there was a difference. It wasn't just the strange food
they ate—beer and overripe bananas, for example—when they
sat around talking. Or bread cooked in water for the children's
breakfast with butter or sugar on top. My new family was
Communist. They were revolutionaries. When in the army,
Pierre's grandfather had poured a bowl of soup on the adjutant's
head because he had said something against workers. Pierre's
father or one of his brothers had done virtually the same thing,
spent time in military prisons, and had his military service
extended—in Indochina yet. They were always talking about
strikes, the dirty bosses, and how they would run things someday. Unknown to me, there was Communist literature in the
attic. When I found it after the war, I wondered what the
Germans would have done had they discovered it during one of
their many searches.

It was all shocking, though on the surface things looked
fine. The six of us lived in a five-room house in Courbevoie on
the western border of Paris. Pierre, the children, and I lived on
the ground floor in a small room off the salon, while his parents
had two bedrooms upstairs, one of them a small sitting room. It
reminded me of Miramas, except that now we had two growing
boys, the house was smaller, and they were Pierre's parents, not
mine. Papa Lemaire went every day to teach his locksmith trade
at the school for Protestant boys run by Pastor Weber. I had
never really met a Protestant before, so when the pastor came to
pay a call I was unnerved until Papa Lemaire introduced us with
his little joke about my Norman produce.

"What, Lucie?" he started. "You've sold your butter and chickens this early in the day?" That was his explanation when I failed to appear with the expected basket.

The pastor was very good to me even though I was Catholic, and so was his son, a classmate of Pierre's before the war. The pastor's son was a doctor, and he always came around to take care of the boys when they were sick. He had also helped Pierre through his divorce and repeated the story of my husband's tears when everything had gone so badly.

I liked these Protestants well enough, but not what came next. My husband's family hated the Church. Nothing about it was good—not the saints, not the Holy Virgin, and especially not the priests. They talked about the fat, old men with rings all over their puffy fingers, wearing silks covered with lace.

"*Le bon Dieu* alone knows what they do all dressed up like that," my father-in-law once said. He suspected the priests who went around among the workers looking poor and thought they were really working for the bosses.

"We've seen that all before—nuns checking out the poor little girls in factories and priests pretending to be like us so they could get our votes."

While Papa Lemaire mocked the processions that had supported my family in Normandy, I set my chin and decided to go to church. I didn't go every Sunday, but when I did, it was early, like Grand-mère, and without any fanfare. Maybe it was then that I picked out my favorite saints. I was sewing a lot for the boys, and would always misplace needles and pins or buttons and my measuring tape. When that happened, I made a quick prayer to Saint Anthony, who had a way of making things turn up. Saint Rita, whose name comes from Marguerite, also became my favorite. She was the patron saint of prostitutes—which wasn't my case of course—but she also helped the unfortunate. Somewhere—was it when Philippe was born, when Maman died, when we became destitute—I began thinking that Saint Rita was the one to whom I would turn.

Life was changing; it always does. Just think—once I had been a spoiled child, now I was a married woman trying to make ends meet. Once I had lived with good Frenchmen, now Communists were my family. Life changed for everyone. After being miserable in the war, people became gay. They did wild dances in Paris, and there were shows where Negro women paraded around almost naked. After the long, elegant dresses of Trouville disappeared, we began wearing short ones. Even underwear changed, especially when Coco Chanel told Frenchwomen to take off their corsets. Before the war women didn't wear brassieres; instead, little fan-like inserts of fine cotton in their corsets covered and pushed up their breasts very prettily. One day when I was talking to a *lingère* in the neighborhood, she warned me that without the support of a brassiere my breasts would soon be hanging around my waist or knees. It's true, you know, as many women of my generation found out. I saved money here and there and bought my first brassiere sometime in the mid-twenties. One thing that didn't change was my love of fashion and my wanting to be up to date.

We all cut our hair. I had four sisters-in-law, and over a period of several weeks there was a parade of bobbed haircuts at my mother-in-law's Sunday dinner. My mother-in-law didn't speak to the first one for almost a month. I was second, and that saved the next two: she had to talk to me because I lived with her. One sister-in-law held out for a few months. Her hair was thick, long, and auburn. Maman Lemaire, almost as if daring her, kept saying that if Simone cut her hair, she would never speak to her again. When it finally happened, my mother-in-law kept her word for almost a year. Only Pierre's and my intervention healed the break. I especially liked the new coiffures because it gave me a chance to experiment with hats for all of us.

My Aunt Suzanne helped keep me up to date with all the changes. Once or twice a year she summoned me to her grand apartment near the Gare St. Lazare. Every time I visited she loaded me with pictures of her children—first the little boy with his long curls and dressed in a sailor suit. He was darling, but so were the two older girls, who always posed together. She usually presented a final picture of the five of them. Uncle Eugène for a while looked sleeker than ever, his hair combed straight back without a part and his mustache now clipped as was the fashion. And Aunt Suzanne was the proud, well-put-together Parisian matron. I most admired her lace encrusted crepe dresses and the long strings of pearls she wore with them.

After the picture ceremony, her maid brought our tea. Aunt Suzanne would then ask about Pierre and the children. But they didn't interest her too much. Most of all she wanted to talk, first about fashion, or her maid or friends, or about her gay life shopping or going to nightclubs. Uncle Eugène was still a pleasure-loving fellow. Too much so, as always became apparent by the end of our conversations, when Aunt Suzanne would break down in tears. Only once in a while would he take her to nightclubs, though he stayed out most nights and rarely came home for dinner at noon. She knew that, like most men, he was chasing women. And I knew that, unlike most women, she was not handling it well.

Pierre liked women, too. But I never nagged him about it because that would only drive him away. I did get after him about smoking and never let up on that. Pierre responded by sneaking out of the house for a cigarette, so much he knew I hated it. Then, of course, the neighbors caught on, and for the rest of his life Mme This or Mme That would come to tell me where she had seen Pierre having a smoke.

As I look back, I don't know whether I was right. Pierre was the best of husbands and worked hard to keep us together and to make sure that each of our boys could learn a trade. For thirteen years, until it folded, he worked at the Delage automobile plant. Cars were becoming the rage and more and more people had them. We never had a car—workers didn't in those days—but we did have our picture taken by one when we had gone for an outing in one of the parks in Paris. There was a lot of money to be made in automobiles, and for a while old man Delage was good at it. People even said that he was a genius, winning many international prizes for his cars. But he didn't pay his workers well. To make ends meet we decided to act as caretakers for a movie theater. That involved opening up the building and cleaning up afterward. The theater was right next to the Banania factory, so the rats who lived off the chocolate and sugar there often made their nests in the theater. After a while the smell from that factory sickened both of us so much that we vowed never to drink hot chocolate again.

Meanwhile old man Delage ruined everything. He, too, chased women, and one in particular—she was either an actress or just his mistress—somehow got all his money. Or at least she diverted him until he went bankrupt, which meant unemployment for Pierre. I can't remember how long it lasted that we only had the little bit from the theater to live on. Then one day we got lucky. Pierre ran into an old comrade who had been on the retreat from Charleroi with him. He was now a foreman at Ford in Pontoise.

"Why don't you come work for us?" he asked. Pierre said that he had already tried Ford and had been turned away. After they chatted for a while he promised to get Pierre in, and he did. There was only one condition.

"We are friends," he said. "But at Ford, you can't *tutoyer* me. You'll have to say *vous* where I'm the foreman, even though nothing will have changed between us."

So Pierre started at Ford and stayed there until his retirement. He took a little train that went from the outskirts of Courbevoie to Pontoise, which meant that instead of coming home at noon, he ate at Ford's canteen. The boys, however, ate their dinners with their grandparents and me. No matter how tight our budget was, I always made sure that there was meat at both meals. My mother-in-law began teaching me to make all the soups and stews that Pierre loved, especially an even better *boeuf à la mode*. For the six of us I would use a kilo and a half of carrots, another of onions, and seven or eight hundred grams of beef. I would add a little garlic (some people didn't, but we liked it), some thyme, a bay leaf, and a knuckle of veal. This made the sauce gelatinous. It smelled so good during the hours it cooked.

I also made my clothes and the boys' as well. They were so close in age that I always dressed them alike, right down to their hand-knitted socks. For their first communion—somewhere about the time they were planning social security—Philippe and Antoine were both outfitted in new sailor suits I had made them. Unfortunately, that was a sad time in an unreligious household. The boys learned their catechism without so much as a word mentioned at home. On the morning of their first communion the four of us got up very early; Pierre and I had breakfast together while the boys went to greet their grandmother—again without saying a thing about the ceremony. After mass we came back in silence and continued as if it were any other day, except that I cooked a leg of lamb. Had everyone celebrated with us, as in most families, the roast would have disappeared. Instead we ate it all week. How unfortunate to have a family like that.

Soon after, Philippe came down with a terrible infection; he coughed blood. The only cure, the doctor said, was to take him away from Paris to the country as quickly as possible. What to do? I asked the neighbors for suggestions about where to go. Secretly, I had put seven hundred francs into a savings account.

"Whatever you do, Madame, " said the butcher's wife with whom I was talking a day later, "don't touch that money. You'll never replace it."

And you know, it was true, but I had to use it. For I had suddenly come up with a plan. I contacted Mme Norman, our old friend from Lisieux, and by return mail she suggested coming to Normandy, where she would find us a place to live.

While Antoine stayed home with his grandmother, Philippe

and I boarded the train for Lisieux.

It wasn't like old times, I can tell you that. But Mme Norman was as good as her word. She had someone meet us at the train and lodged us with a good woman in a town not too far from the château. We could only stay two weeks, my purse was so flat. One day my landlady was watching me work on some school clothes for the boys.

"You know, Madame, you sew very well," she said.

"Do you think so, Madame?" I answered.

"It's too bad, for the young man's sake, you can't stay in the country longer." That was my thought too, and even under these conditions it was good to be in Normandy.

"Do you think you could do some sewing for me? And I imagine the innkeeper might also have some work. That way you could stay a little longer."

That's the way it was done. The next summer I took both boys to another country place belonging to the family of my Uncle Jacques. There was no stove, no electricity. Having learned a bit the value of my sewing, I negotiated with several of the neighboring landowners. One exchanged firewood and a little meat; another produce. That way we had the country air all for the cost of our train tickets.

When I try to think of what happened in Courbevoie, there isn't much interesting to tell. It was gray in comparison to Normandy and the south. Is that the difference, I wonder, between being young, sewing hats, falling in love and living, middle-aged, in a factory town? We had our little amusements, like going to the greyhound races. We had our neighborhood gossip too, especially about the concierge of a building a few houses down. Concierges have always had bad reputations of one sort or another. They spread rumors or spied on tenants, interfered in others' business, or led disreputable lives. Some were in thick with the police; the concierge in question was in thick with our mailman.

One day she called to me as I passed her building. "You must know a good doctor, Madame," she said winking. I gave her the name of Pastor Weber's son. Several days later she accosted me again, only this time she was angry. She had wanted an abortion; Doctor Weber would do no more than tell her what she already knew: she was pregnant. By coincidence, the mailman's wife gave birth to a child at the same time the concierge did. Everyone said the two babies looked identical. It did nothing but add to the reputation of concierges.

In those days such goings-on were small diversions. We had more important matters to think about—namely the future of Philippe and Antoine. Pierre and I saved. I took in sewing so that, as we had long ago promised each other, they could each study a trade. Philippe learned about boilerworks, and Antoine about cabinetmaking. It seemed then that both could earn a good livelihood with those skills.

Sometime during the boys' apprenticeships we began getting paid vacations. Léon Blum was the premier who gave them to us, and from that moment on workers could see a little bit of the country. It wasn't until 1939 that we got to take advantage of the new program by going with my mother-in-law to Cancale. Having visited there for more than twenty summers, she thought of it as a second home. Even though Cancale was in Brittany and the beach was rocky, for me it meant returning to the sea. It had not changed in twenty-five years, but the rest of us had—our clothes, our habits, my way of life.

How can I forget Cancale? We were there when the war broke out. Pierre was called back immediately to Ford; and the boys, who had done their military training, were called up for active duty. They called it the "phony war" for a while, but that didn't last forever. Pierre put in good hours at Ford; the boys came home on leave occasionally. I remember one thought in particular from those years: for the first and only time I wished that I had had daughters instead of sons.

We had one problem to complicate an already bad situation. Antoine loved to chase women when he was on leave. The trouble—and it became an even bigger trouble than we then suspected—had begun when he was sixteen. I would hear from the neighbors of a little Suzette or Marie with whom he had been seen; sometimes I would even see one of them myself, waiting near our house for Antoine to walk by. Philippe was much more serious in this respect. Nanette, whose family lived a few streets away, was the only girl who appealed to him. Not so with Antoine, who used his uniform to attract more and more women. I complained to Pierre, but all he said was that boys would be boys.

Then everything collapsed and the Germans came. I remember the radio telling us not to panic—don't leave Paris—your government will protect you. Ford knew better than that, although most of us didn't for a week or so. All the workers and their families were evacuated to Bordeaux, and who was there too but the entire French government! I can't remember what I took in the rush, except that I packed some silverware, my goblets from Maman, and other things into suitcases. For some reason I also carried a pink and white blanket.

When the defeat came, Ford workers were sent back to the plants. Pierre left and we stayed behind, first with a family near Bordeaux, then we moved near Châteauroux. In November, Pierre sent a passport and said that we should come back. By that time Philippe had found Antoine and me; together we waited two nights in the station before a train came that we were allowed to board.

At Vierzon the soldiers made people get off the trains. Thinking that they only wanted heads of families, I left the boys to go present our papers myself. Behind me I could hear everyone being sent off, and from the corner of my eye I glimpsed my sons sent with a crowd down a completely different route from my own. I panicked, until, reboarding the train, I heard them calling.

How do you talk about things like this, and how do you tell people who never lived through it what feelings one had? It's impossible, so I don't talk about the war, except to say one thing. Marshall Pétain saved my sons. De Gaulle—he left us. Had my sons done the same thing, they would have been shot. But the marshall stayed with us even though he was an old man. He came to an agreement with the Germans and kept my sons from being killed. And I've never hesitated to say this to anyone.

It was a long trip to Paris for the three of us, especially because we never knew what might happen. Could we ever stop watching or being ready for something, we didn't know what? Finally people started recognizing the outskirts of the city, and at about 10:00 P.M. we arrived at the Gare d'Austerlitz. But there it was again—10:00 P.M. curfew. The station was fairly deserted. We could either stay the night, which was forbidden, or make our way like criminals through the equally forbidden streets to Courbevoie—almost on the other side of the city. Of course, we did the latter, so determined were the three of us to see our home after five months.

The first familiar house in Courbevoie we came to was Nanette's on the Rue de Verdun. Everyone came to meet us even though it was after midnight.

"Poor Madame," Nanette embraced me. "Monsieur Lemaire has been at the station every night for a week. And you arrive tonight when he was too discouraged to make the trip."

While we were telling our story, Pierre arrived, and what a reunion we had. Even our dog was there, dancing around. We had more than one reason to be happy. It had been decreed that all dogs should be shot, but the allocation of bullets had run out before his turn came around.

After that our thoughts centered mostly on the boys. In order to get ration coupons they had to register with the government, and eventually they had to go with the rest to do service for Germany. Philippe went to Austria to do farmwork, while Antoine headed for the Daimler-Benz factory in Stuttgart. The family Philippe stayed with treated him well, and

living on a farm solved the problem of his appetite. But Antoine was not so fortunate. We lived for any notes, which came
through fairly often in the first years, and we lived for the
annual holiday they could take.

What days those were! No one had a *crise de foie* [liver
attack] during the war, I can assure you of that. Except the
butchers. They always looked healthy and wouldn't give a gram
more than the ration card allowed. And who knows what was in
the pâté we ate—no one's stomach could allow thinking about
that. One stood in line forever and for everything—even for
horrible wooden-soled shoes. My hair turned gray in 1940, and
I dyed it ash blond. Standing in line one day I heard someone
say: "What good is it to have beautifully colored hair when it's
full of lice?" And it was true—lots of people like us had them,
and fleas as well. But there was little to be done without good
soap. After that I always wore a scarf to go shopping.

The boys were continually on our minds. Philippe came
back from Austria and announced that he and Nanette were
getting married. I remembered my mother's rule about no
romance in wartime. But things had changed, or maybe I never
believed in the rule at all. Why stop the young from having
a moment's pleasure?—was my husband's opinion. He knew
what war was. So they went ahead, without the morning suits
and top hats, without gowns and trousseaus, and certainly
without a three-day wedding feast. Searching for some means to
celebrate, I suddenly remembered our old friend Mme Norman,
who sent a roast beef and rabbits from Normandy.

One thing about the wedding made me smile though it was
wartime. My mother-in-law went to the religious ceremony in
what may have been her first entry into a church since her
marriage into an atheist family. The rest was sad. Philippe had
to leave after two weeks because five co-workers, the authorities
said, would be shot if he failed to return to Austria. A month
after his departure Nanette announced that she was pregnant.

Antoine had his leave just before Nanette's baby was due.

Madame Lucie's Story

He was smiling, sporting a tattoo, and pursuing young women from the minute he set foot in Courbevoie. Everyone, of course, was starved for love. So it wasn't just the tattoo that made Antoine an object of attention.

I remembered seeing a tattooed woman in the circus at Caen. Unlike Antoine, whose picture was merely a heart on his forearm, unlike Pierre's grandfather, who had a portrait of the Empress Eugénie on his chest, this circus woman had been covered, every visible inch of her, with blue emblems. They say that tattoos can be removed by retracing the pictures with a needle dipped in mother's milk.

In any case, Antoine's gallivanting lasted only a short time. He suddenly had an attack of appendicitis and we rushed him to a hospital in Neuilly. No sooner was Antoine on the road to recovery than Nanette went into labor. At a clinic several blocks from Antoine she gave us our first grandchild, Michel, born June 22, 1943. You see how life is full of coincidences: my parents were married on June 22. I had hoped for a different name for the baby, but for some reason Michel was fashionable then.

Back and forth I walked between the two hospitals. Antoine's leave was running out, so we had Pastor Weber's son write for a medical leave. In spite of that we began getting letters from the German authorities demanding his return; Doctor Weber wrote more letters. Things became even more troublesome. Not only did we have a new baby to worry about, but Antoine, who now seemed as fit as a fiddle, started taking up with the neighborhood women. He had no sense of caution, only of pleasure.

Sometime later that summer we received a notice to report *with Antoine* to the military headquarters in Paris. I can tell you what we felt—only the worst. I insisted on going alone—my husband couldn't tell a lie, and besides he had seen his brother killed by the Germans. His whole family was too rebellious to be trusted. So I set out for the Place de la Concorde, where the headquarters was. After waiting only a few minutes a soldier ushered me into the office in charge of French laborers.

"Where is your son?"

"Why, *Monsieur le Général*, he is home recovering from bad appendicitis and can't travel," I replied as meekly as possible.

"Appendicitis lasts a long time in this country."

"It is a very serious illness."

"Madame Lemaire, make sure that your son reports" (I can't remember how long he gave us but let's say) "in three weeks."

"Yes, *Monsieur le Général*." He then signaled that I could leave. But as I started to open the door, he said one more thing.

"Make sure you're clear about this, Mme Lemaire. If he isn't here in three weeks, I will have him shot."

My hand froze to the doorknob, and for a moment I couldn't move. When Antoine heard this report, his cavalier attitude disappeared. After packing a few things he started out for Chambord, where he hoped to be able to hide with the wood-cutters in the forest. He would never return to Daimler-Benz. His German foreman, who had given Antoine money to bring back French suspenders, is waiting for them still.

When our grace period was up (and thinking about it again, it must have been less than three weeks), gendarmes began filling the house at random moments, night and day. For ten days or so they searched for him relentlessly, and then, just as suddenly as they appeared, their pursuit stopped. But though the invasion of our house had ended, our hearts were still tortured. There was the baby and Nanette, whom the authorities had not spared in the search. Then all communication from Philippe stopped; we were not to hear from him until the end of the war. To complete our anxiety, or so it seemed then, Antoine, having somehow heard that the search for him had relented, appeared on our doorstep late one evening.

How reckless, I thought at the time. He seemed to have no sense of danger at all, though at least he didn't stay with us.

Instead he used the hospitality of all the young women friends he had in Courbevoie. Occasionally I would hear that he had been seen with one of them, walking in broad daylight as if he weren't almost a dead man. The consequences weren't long in coming, for people in those days behaved desperately and badly. One day a woman, a toddler in tow, knocked at my door. I had seen her somewhere in the area, but I couldn't place her exactly.

"Madame," she said, "I've been seeing a lot of your son, even hiding him. But now I'm telling you what I've told him. If he doesn't marry me soon, I'll denounce him to the Gestapo."

Again my blood froze; there's no other way to put it. Didn't all of us know that people were actually doing such things? News had reached us even from the little village of St. Pars les Vaud, where I had taken the boys for summers, that one woman had denounced (I believe it was) the grocer woman, for some small jealousy, and the grocer woman had been shot.

When Antoine made his next visit, Pierre became very serious with our son as we all tried to think of a solution—and quickly. Antoine finally decided to head south and enlist in the army of Algeria. Marrying—publicly—was out of the question for a fugitive, and besides, the woman in question was frivolous beyond words. On the other hand, Pierre had had enough of his son's frivolity, which was jeopardizing all of us. For the first time he gave Antoine an ultimatum.

"You may have some years to work this out, and while you are in Algeria find yourself a wife. Marry an Indian, marry a Negress, but don't come back unless you are married."

We were not yet out of danger—in fact, we were heading for more as 1943 passed. Because of the heavy industry everyone in Courbevoie felt that the suburb was an even more dangerous place to be than Paris. My husband and I decided that I would go to the country with Nanette and the baby. I earned our keep, while Nanette minded him. The news from Paris was not good. The British were bombing everywhere, even Caen. They turned the city into a rubble heap and I would never forgive them for that. Paris, we heard, had been mined by the Germans. And as if we didn't have enough trouble heaped on us by our enemies, the British were destroying France with their planes.

Still, the countryside provided some peace of mind, for there was plenty to eat. A tiny town near Le Mans was one where my Aunt Suzanne had connections, so we were well received. The inhabitants were more than willing to sell us whatever they had in the way of dairy products and game. The first week there I was able to send Pierre a pheasant, and he reciprocated by sending us coal. In fact, a few weeks later he was standing by our outdoor coal cellar preparing to send me more supplies when the planes flew over, suddenly dropping bombs on Courbevoie. Pierre found cover and was unhurt, but our house caught fire. He sent a message to me the next day.

All I could think of was being homeless again. We would have even less than ever. Whatever would we do—my husband and I, our sons and grandchildren? I hurried back, leaving Nanette and the baby with the good people of Bonnétable. Our first solution—what everyone said to do—was go to the housing office in Paris near the Opéra. It meant standing in a line made very long by the bombings. When we reached the head of it, a French woman representing the Germans asked:

"Do you work for us?"

"*Oui*, Madame," I answered. Everyone worked for the Germans in those days, though no one will admit it now.

She gave us an address in the eleventh arrondissement along with a handful of papers to give the concierge, and we walked for an hour to get there, down the boulevards, past the Place de la République. We saw the Bastille monument in the distance; I had never seen it or visited this part of Paris before. At the Place Voltaire we asked for directions; just a few blocks more and we reached the Rue Basfroi.

The concierge was not overjoyed to see refugees coming

into her building. And when a few days later she said that
the apartment belonged to some Jewish people who had been
deported, I wasn't overjoyed either. They would probably be
back, I thought; our housing problem hadn't ended.

In the meantime I decided to find out about the neighborhood, which was unusual to say the least. Little workshops
everywhere, furniture makers, cabinetmakers, clothing. It
didn't bustle exactly—nothing did in those days except the big
plants outside the city. I met a family of clothing manufacturers
down the street a bit who were on their way out of town until
things quieted down. Within two days of our meeting this same
Mme Rosenberg gave me the keys to her apartment and the
Mon Tricot workshop she owned with instructions to watch
them if I could. She promised to reward me if everything went
well.

Pierre and I both tried to find odd jobs. In that area it wasn't
too difficult, given that we were both hard workers and that I
could sew for these people who had sewing of all kinds to do.
For me, there was the other problem of finding food when
grocers only cared for their long-standing customers. But walking blocks, standing in line, I came to know the *quartier* and the
people.

One day, in line at the Place Voltaire, the concierge at
3 Passage des Chats, just around the corner from our place,
struck up a conversation. We started in about what was avail-
able at the market that day, then I told her about our uncertain
housing.

"Why, Madame," she said, "the baron who owns the building needs someone to care for the other half of it."

"You mean to say he needs a concierge?"

"Why, yes. There's a good little *loge* for you and your
husband."

My heart sank at the humiliation of it all. Hauling garbage
cans, cleaning common toilets, serving as the butt of ridicule
and intrigue—that's what the future as a concierge would hold.

But I took the address of Mme Poncet, who managed all the baron's property. That afternoon she and I met for the first time. Apparently having confidence in me, Mme Poncet hired me on the spot.

For once I was glad that my parents were dead and couldn't see what had become of me. I was never raised to be a concierge.

Part II

Madame Lucie Observed

4

A Parisian Concierge

Paris, 1976

Never was a street better named than the Passage des Chats.
Low-slung city cats roamed the sidewalk, the open courtyards,
and stairs. They sunned themselves on the metal roofs of sheds
where artisans kept their tools and motorbikes. No one appreciated them less than Mme Lucie, now hunched over as if looking
for the messes they left everywhere.

Two doors protected the entrance to the concierge's *loge*.
The interior one was always open when the weather was as good
as it was that June day; the outer one, divided in two horizontally, was open at the top, so that Mme Lucie could peer into
the courtyard and entryway like a sentinel. Leaning on the
bottom half, she watched old Mme Perrugia vigorously limping
toward her, cane in one hand, pocketbook in the other. The
concierge hailed her with an epithet about the cats.

"Well now you have four more, Madame," her tenant
responded. Their mother just gave birth in the hall sink on the
third floor. Showing her disgust, Mme Perrugia paused for Mme
Lucie's reaction.

Madame Lucie Observed

"What a misery. What am I going to do?" She couldn't, it was clear, march upstairs and take care of them herself. At eighty, she could hardly see because of detached retinas in both eyes. She shuffled out into the courtyard to show Mme Perrugia how feeble her gait was from rheumatism in both hips.

"Kill them for me, Madame," she pleaded feebly, adding that she wouldn't be able to tell kittens from the sink itself. "After all these years you could do me this one service."

To alleviate the problems caused by Mme Lucie's infirmities, Mme Perrugia would do some of her shopping or run little errands. She kept her company when things were slow. But after many years of such cajoling Mme Perrugia also knew resistance. Now she was being asked to commit murder, and she refused.

"Ugh, I couldn't kill the little things, but I'll bring them down to you." Madame Perrugia started toward the stairs. Almost eighty herself, she was Mme Lucie's other half, physically energetic when something had to be done.

It was Sunday afternoon in the Passage des Chats. No furniture men dragged their loads of chairs; the printing presses had stopped their clicking; and the few families who lived instead of worked in the building were either sealed in their apartments for the day or had left the city to find fresh air. The courtyard was tranquil, except for the noise of water from the sink, filling Mme Lucie's bucket.

Madame Perrugia thumped loudly again down the stairs, a full plastic sack trailing next to her cane.

"I scared the mother off with a good swing of my purse. Now they're all yours." She turned to walk out on the street.

"No, you can't leave now. I can't do this myself. Hand them to me one at a time." Madame Lucie took each kitten as it was presented, held it in the bucket for several minutes, then returned it to her friend.

"Put them back in the sack. This last one doesn't want to cooperate." She immersed the kitten a second time, deposited it in the sack, and then put the corpses carefully in the garbage can facing the *loge*.

"Whatever you do, don't mention a word about kittens to Marie-Louise. She'll ransack the building for them and make our lives miserable. What a Sunday!" Regaining her composure, if indeed she had ever lost it, Mme Lucie said good-bye to her accomplice and returned to lean on the half-door of the *loge*.

Of all the habitués of the Passage des Chats, Mme Marie-Louise was one of the strangest, if the most appropriate. Every evening between eight and ten she appeared, thin and witch-like, a wicker basket in one hand, assorted plastic bags in the other. Depending on her point of entry to the small street, she stopped first at number one, then at number three, and spread a layer of newspapers on the sidewalk. Passersby who gave a polite greeting received one in return, along with comments on the weather or the plight of cats. If, however, the observer looked disapproving or grunted at her efforts, Mme Marie-Louise, her stringy gray hair falling straight around her face, could be heard to mumble rhythmically as she set out cans of food and plates of milk on the ersatz tablecloths.

"I put a curse on people who don't like cats," she explained to Mme Lucie.

So as the evening of the drownings fell, the concierge leaned characteristically on the half-door with some apprehension. Just as characteristically she appeared to be staring into space, innocent of the world's cruelty and crime. Mme Marie-Louise's greeting jolted her mocked tranquillity.

"Why, Mme Marie-Louise, I thought you had been here already. It's wretched to be so feeble and almost sightless."

Instead of responding, the cat-woman set to work in her usual manner, while the cats appeared in a desultory fashion, so habituated were they to a meal materializing at nightfall. By the time everything was in place, more than a dozen cats had taken up stations, with others on their way.

The cat-woman made ready to move down the Passage. "Keep an eye out for our little mother to be, won't you Mme Lemaire. I'll be back to clean all this up." She left with Mme Lucie's sweet assurances of concern for the pregnant cat trailing after her.

"What a crazy woman," the concierge mumbled in turn. Without waiting for a return engagement, she pushed aside the geraniums, closed the shutters on the windows to the *loge*, and went to bed.

Monday morning at eight the first mail of the day arrived at the Passage des Chats. A few minutes before, an American woman had entered the *loge* to hear the gruesome events of the previous day.

"It's terrible to be old," Mme Lucie started. "Look at me. I used to go to my children's for Sunday dinner. Before that, they came here, and in the old days we feasted at my grandmother's. Now Sunday I have to kill cats because I can't eat my daughter-in-law's food, can't see to walk there, can't even walk that far if I could see.

"*You* know I have nothing against the poor animals, who for all that they're pests keep the mice and rats out of the building. If you were to go over to where *les grands* live—say to the baron's neighborhood—you'd find rats everywhere."

The American agreed, adding a story of her recent visit to an apartment near the Parc Monceau, where rats swarmed around garbage cans in the evening.

"Madame Marie-Louise doesn't care about the turds on the stairs, in the courtyards, and even in the sinks. She likes cats better than people, better than her husband who left her because the cats filled their apartment." Madame Lucie buttressed her conviction that Marie-Louise was a monomaniac with a story about the time she found a cat missing from the bodycount. The telephone men having just finished filling in trenches three feet deep for replacing cables, she decided that the missing cat had been buried and that the trenches should be dug out to find it. "You can imagine what they said to her!" For her part Marie-Louise stormed around cursing them.

"Really, the neighborhood was in an uproar. It has been ever since she started feeding those cats."

"Perhaps you could explain to her that the cats are upsetting the tenants," the American suggested.

"My goodness no. Just the other day I mentioned that some people didn't like the way she was encouraging the cats by feeding them. She said she would put a curse on them, and she would put one on me, I can assure you."

The mailman's knock interrupted Mme Lucie's recital of all the curses the cat-woman had pronounced in recent years. Pushing open the half-door, he greeted the two women.

"*Bonjour*, Mesdames. How beautiful my day is when it starts off with two such lovely ladies." He offered his hand to Mme Rogers, slid over to Mme Lucie's side of the room, and shook hers.

"*Bonjour*, mailman. What interesting things do you have?" She tried to address him. But the mailman was full of himself, adjusting his cap, smoothing the front of his uniform, as he strutted the short distance of the room.

"You know, Madame," he winked at the concierge, "I hear that American women easily fall in love with Frenchmen. Do you think that's true?"

"It's possible, but I don't think they would fall in love with anyone with a reputation for being a philanderer." Madame Lucie was being surprisingly rude, but then the mailman had just stopped his parade very close to Mme Rogers's chair. "Now what mail do you have?"

"A great bundle today, Madame, and you owe me one franc."

The concierge reached into her pocket and deposited a handful of change on the table.

"Take what is owed you. I can't see enough to count the right amount." And with that the mailman proceeded to take close to three francs.

"Just right, Madame. We are square. Unfortunately, I have to leave, but I could return if anyone wanted to chat some more." With that he left the *loge*, saluting and bowing in the process.

"A woman-chaser of the first rank," was Mme Lucie's comment. Most men go after women, she explained, even her husband had, but the mailman was extraordinary. He had a reputation for being thick with one concierge or another in the neighborhood.

"But how could a concierge get away with it?" Mme Rogers wondered out loud. There were always people in and out of the *loge*, deliverymen, tenants, visitors, bureaucrats.

"People can get away with anything these days. Look at Mme Rosa in the next building. She and this mailman were a couple for months, right under her husband's nose. And someday, I'll tell you what she did before that—very spectacular. Of course, I don't see these things and I don't ask. People just bring stories to me when they need to chat. That's another job of the concierge—to listen. Anyway, we'd better get to our work." Leaving Mme Rosa (the handsome concierge in the other half of the building) unexplained, Mme Lucie began untying the bundle of mail. She slipped the cord into a drawer and handed the letters to Mme Rogers, who started reading the names.

"Madame Bernard."

"Put that in the right hand corner of the table," said the old woman.

"Monsieur Dupin."

"Ah, he will be happy—probably an order or a check. Put that in front of me."

The sorting continued in its usual way. Madame Rogers read, while Mme Lucie positioned the letters in a special part of the table. Because at eighty she could no longer read even with her magnifying glass, by assigning names to various locations she could deliver the mail to the proper tenant.

"Monsieur Cailloux."

"Who is that from?" When Mme Rogers announced that it was from the social security, Mme Lucie began to fret. Monsieur Cailloux had injured himself at the Renault factory, but to collect workman's compensation he had to be at home for the visit of the agency's inspector.

"The poor man has gone to the country to rest. When the inspector came by the other day, I said he had gone to the doctor. I'll have to call and warn him. Always these busybodies. The same thing happened when my unfortunate husband first had his heart trouble."

Madame Rogers continued the mail call. Her unofficial job had begun almost a year before, when at 8:15 one morning she had run down to get the mail. Mme Lucie had been struggling with her magnifying glass and a letter.

"Come in, *ma petite dame*. Could you read this name for me? And maybe two or three others." The next day had been the same, except that Mme Rogers read an additional two or three. Within a week she was doing the entire delivery.

"It's terrible to be old, and above all not to be able to see clearly. My poor mother died before this happened to her, only forty-seven years old. But people are so good to me. Monsieur Robert, the printer, does my eyedrops. One night he stopped by just to chat a bit—you see, he has a friend in the next building—you know her, the brunette with the little dog. Anyway, I asked if he would mind counting out my eyedrops, and since then he hasn't missed a single evening except during vacation. I hate being dependent on people—like Madame Gourdin for my shopping or Monsieur Garbaud for the stairs. But that is old age."

At that point the door to the *loge* opened brusquely and in walked Monsieur Dupin, the chair merchant.

"*Bonjour*, Mesdames. What do you have for me?"

"Ah, Monsieur Dupin, the little American here has found you all sorts of treasures," the concierge replied.

He looked quickly at his mail and left, muttering sourly about receiving nothing but bills.

"Don't worry about him," the concierge said to Mme Rogers. "He's rich as Croesus."

"Still," said the American, "it must be nice to get checks instead of bills."

"And nice for me also," replied the concierge. "The artisans are much more pleasant when business is good and they give better tips. I didn't always have to worry like this; it seems another lifetime when I played the piano and wore white gloves and beautiful hats. But here I am keeping you from going to work, and I must deliver the mail to keep them happy."

"Yes, I should get off to business," and the American started to leave.

"If it's not asking too much, do you think you could pay me a little visit tonight? These months beginning with J give me dark thoughts."

The American said she would try, knowing like most others in the building that Mme Lucie's wishes were hard to refuse. With a handshake, they parted, the concierge arranging the mail in its usual order—two letters for Monsieur Mesta, one for Perrugia, stairway A; then stairway B, then C. In her bathrobe, seeing little, she still knew everything about her building and its inhabitants.

For everyone in the Passage des Chats except Mme Lucie, June was a particularly good month. Parisians hadn't left the city for summer vacations, orders were still coming in. The nice weather allowed the artisans to work almost in fresh air, so light and breezy were the workshops once the enormous windows could be swung open. And there was no carrying heavy loads of chairs and cabinets, of clothing and handbags in the rain or sleet. Instead, there was an atmosphere of carnival, complete with organ-grinder who strolled the neighborhood. Stealing a moment when their bosses' backs were turned, the younger workmen would hang out windows or stand in doorways to watch for a passing female and to be rewarded when Colette, Mme Lucie's stunning granddaughter, left for her job in the Métro.

At noon the cafés on the Rue de Charonne or Charles d'Alléry filled with artisans, pipe and cigarette smoke, the clinking of glasses and silverware, the Passage des Chats itself being too tiny for any such establishments. Besides, the Passage, no longer than a hundred yards, was entirely taken up on one side by the converted Napoleonic barracks over which Mmes Luce and Rosa presided and on the other by two new apartment buildings.

"When I first moved here," Mme Lucie often told newcomers, "the other side was just sheds and a couple of workshops. The street wasn't even paved, and people got in the habit of walking their dogs. I guess that's the only thing that hasn't changed in the neighborhood: the dogs still do their business on our street."

That night when Mme Rogers stopped in at the *loge*, the day in the building was on the concierge's mind. Madame Lucie was leaning on the half-door looking at the garbage cans in the courtyard, but actually waiting for the visit.

"Ah, my faithful friend. I thought you had forgotten this poor old woman."

"I'm sorry, Madame, but the children were in an uproar."

"Well, things are in an uproar here as well. Madame Bellini died—right in her apartment—and the ambulance and police came and poor old Monsieur Bellini who is almost my age has gone off in grief. The poor people—here since before I arrived and now carried away in an ambulance. But she was right, that woman, not to go to the hospital—you live much longer if you wait for the end at home. I often think, Madame, that if my husband hadn't gone to the hospital—fifteen years ago this very month—he would still be with me today."

"You may be right, Mme Lucie," said Mme Rogers, "but the doctors like to have you right there in case of emergency."

"Let's not dwell on such things. It gives me bad ideas. Tell me what you did today." For the past two years their conversations always started with Mme Lucie politely inquiring about the American's day, what she had had for lunch, what she had seen. They would both do their knitting, and Mme Lucie would be concerned about its progress.

This evening ritual had begun two years earlier in the hottest July in memory. The heat was unbearable, and Mme Rogers's family had left for the country while she stayed to work. If the world ever ends, she remembered thinking, it will be this way—hot and airless. She set out to get a cold drink at a café, as her refrigerator had broken with the onset of the heat wave.

As she passed the concierge's *loge*, she met the Sister Marie-Ste. Geneviève, looking worried.

"*Bonsoir*, Madame. Where are you going?" the sister asked.

"Just for a walk, *ma soeur*," the American lied. "My family has left on vacation and I need to . . ."

"Madame Lemaire is very sick. Her children are on vacation and I was just going to get another sister to relieve me." Sister Marie-Ste. Geneviève belonged to the Sisters of Charity—an order that had its hands full in this neighborhood. "Could you stay with Mme Lemaire until the doctor comes? We are so busy and understaffed, what with half the sisters on vacation."

The American agreed and entered the *loge*. It was a small room whose space was taken up by a large round table always covered with red and white flowered oilcloth, a buffet with pictures of Saint Theresa of Lisieux and the concierge's two boys and two silver goblets, and an armoire of undetermined contents. A tiny kitchen was off to the right, and past that an alcove where the concierge lay in a huge double bed that filled the tiny area. Mme Rogers approached it and saw, instead of a concierge who lifted garbage cans and ran a building of forty apartments, what appeared to be a cadaver. Madame Lucie's teeth were out, and her usually curly white hair lay damp and yellowish on her scalp.

"Excuse me, Madame, the sister has asked me to sit with you until the doctor comes. Do you mind?"

"Ah, she too thinks I'm going to die. No, it will be nice if you sit here, but won't Monsieur, your husband, want you at home?"

As Mme Rogers began explaining, the doctor made his majestic appearance. In uniform he wore a pin-striped gray jacket like a morning coat, black trousers, spats and gray gloves. An oiled mustache, veiled eyelids, and marcelled hair made him look like a character in a French farce. The voice was stereotypically and reassuringly authoritarian.

"*Mesdames!* What is going on here?"

"Ah, *Monsieur le docteur*," the concierge's voice had become weak, whining, and obsequious. "This will probably be the last time you have to take care of me." Madame Rogers gave her place over quickly to Doctor Mourant. She could hear the sheets moving, the doctor asking a question or two, and then . . .

"Am I dying? Should I call my children back from vacation?"

"Not at all, Madame, but we're going to put you in the hospital. You need some tests."

"Oh, I can't go, Doctor. Too much to be done here."

"And just how are you going to get along?"

"Well, you can have the laboratory people come do their work here. The sisters can come during the day, and Mme Rogers can come in the evening. She said that her family is gone for a while."

And so it happened that the sisters began coming every day to take care of Mme Lucie; after the emergency had passed, they gave her backrubs and injections for her arthritis. Mme Rogers, too, watched over the sickbed where the concierge lay, looking sick indeed for a week, but gradually better—the first sign being on the fourth day the appearance of Mme Lucie's withered form in a lacy silken nightgown.

"I made it years ago when my husband was still alive. I was buxom then—and now look at me, my breasts down to my stomach. That comes from not wearing brassieres when one is young." Madame Lucie was in a voluble mood, so she launched a discussion of fashion.

"At the top of the corset, one placed inserts of mousseline that made a woman's chest very pretty and soft-looking. Women knew how to look beautiful in those days. Today no one has any style." For about an hour she continued talking about some of the costumes she had seen at Trouville.

"Even the gentlemen were superb."

"I'm afraid I'm tiring you and had better leave," Mme Rogers prepared to go.

"But you will come back tomorrow. Evenings are so lonely, especially in July—an awful month. My father died then, my husband too."

"I'll try to make it tomorrow, and you can tell me more stories."

"There, I knew you'd like them because you like France. What I'm telling you is the history of France."

With that, Mme Lucie had set the routine of their evening meetings, just as, using other arguments, she had scheduled several women in the apartment to visits during the day. They had all been seduced, or at least Mme Rogers felt she had been, into sitting with the old woman on that balmy June evening two years later.

"I'll tell you, Madame, it's hard on me to see people go after thirty years. Come and go, come and go. That's all life is these days. When I first moved in, everyone was French—except for Mme Perrugia—and everyone was an artisan, mostly cabinet-makers. Now the building is a Tower of Babel and the rest of the neighborhood looks more like Algeria than Paris."

"Do you like changes, Madame?" The American asked,

almost knowing what the response would be. She had seen Mme Lucie struggling with three or four American tenants who could barely speak French, with the Yugoslav family, the Spanish, the Italians. Only the Swiss artist spoke her language correctly, but even he was a problem. "A disagreeable person," Mme Lucie had pronounced him after he had accused her of holding back mail he was expecting.

"The Americans are very nice and always good to me, like you, Madame," the concierge smiled coquettishly at her companion. "But you know they are a little scatterbrained. Monsieur Harton, for example. He never locks his door, he invites people from everywhere to stay with him. One day seven people with sleeping bags came trooping in trying to find his apartment. They hardly spoke a word of French between them—but I knew where to send them. When we got to his apartment on the fourth floor, I could tell he had no idea who they were—but in they went."

Everyone in the neighborhood recognized Harton because he had been the first of the Americans to find the hidden street, maybe even to discover that Paris existed east of the Place de la Bastille. A smiling Californian, Harton, his wife, and four children had paid their money under the table to Mme Poncet, the baron's agent, and then registered with her as a marionette maker.

"A marionette maker?" one of his guests had laughed.

"Sure, everyone in this building has a nineteenth-century occupation. You see that snooty Mme Bernard—she is a flower maker. Each workshop has to be occupied forever by successors to the trade. The French are crazy."

Except Harton didn't think they were crazy in fact. He loved their savvy and style. After a trip to the Faubourg St. Germain he would return exuberant.

"Best-looking women in the world. Incredible to think of them working for hours on their clothes, hours in front of the mirror just to parade down a street."

Madame Lucie Observed

But Harton, when he practiced his own métier, when he painted, didn't always chose the Faubourg St. Germain. Instead he recorded the parts of Paris on their way out—the *cafés-charbon* that used to supply the neighborhoods with coal, about to be converted into medium-priced restaurants or the old walls where new apartments were going up. His greatest coup was a series of Les Halles paintings done both before the huge, central market was torn down, and then during the demolition process.

"Someday I'll make a fortune from these," he calculated. It was Harton's magic that unlike most artists in the unfashionable parts of the city, he actually lived from his painting. At least once and sometimes twice a year he headed for the United States with fifty or a hundred canvases in his baggage.

"He produces paintings the way Scott produces toilet paper, and they're just about as good," was the sculptor's assessment. "He sells them in the same way, too." The sculptor, David, was not from Harton's part of town. Being a descendant of the world's most famous oil family, he lived in a two-story flat overlooking the Seine near the Eiffel Tower. He dressed in blue jeans and his maids wore uniforms.

Harton replied in kind. "David's just the kind of guy I sell to in the States. A friend, say in Washington, will arrange an art party, and all his buddies with their fat wallets will show up. I take my shoes off and spread canvases out in the living room, den, dining room floor. Sometimes I make them take their shoes off, too. They think they're buying cute scenes of Paris; they're too dumb to know it's art. Except—the higher I put the price, the better they think the painting is."

Harton always returned to Paris, glad to be back to the French style and a place where he, like most expatriates, could feel his freedom by not belonging to the society. Though stopped now and then by the police for his eccentric ways, he had exulted, especially in May 1968, riding his motorcycle around the fringes of the action. That was when he painted the courtyard walls with portraits of Mme Lucie.

A *Parisian* Concierge

"The sons of bitches plastered them over when they finally came to this part of town to execute the government's orders about cleaning all Parisian buildings—great paintings of my greatest subject." Harton raved about the concierge.

"There she stands every day, leaning over the door. She says she sees nothing—I'll tell you she sees everything. She complains about being helpless—I'll testify under oath that she could run this whole damned country. In June of sixty-eight, when the garbage hadn't been collected for six weeks, they sent the army in to scrape off the big streets. Well, she knew they'd be passing down the Rue Charonne or at least down the Faubourg St. Antoine, and somehow she got to them. Just imagine yourself a young soldier and you see this little white-haired old lady hobbling toward you, and she asks you a favor, 'Come over, *Messieurs les soldats*, please take our garbage because I'm blind and old and the baron will put me out on the street if it doesn't get taken away.' You feel touched as if your grandmother were going to be evicted. So you get the truck to make a detour of a few blocks, and as she gives you orders about not missing this and pick up that, you and your buddies realize that she's no grandmother, she's a god-damned general. I know, I watched the whole business at about six in the morning, not believing what I saw—the French army obeying a concierge. When it was cleaned to her satisfaction, she turned all grandmotherly again and brought out a few bottles of wine for them. We were the only building for blocks that didn't stink, which only goes to prove that Mme Lucie is a powerful woman. But if you don't like watching old people, keep an eye on the granddaughter, Colette."

The wonders Mme Lucie could work on the police, with government employees, on bureaucrats in the *mairie* [arrondissement town hall], with utility repairmen, were pieces of lore that newcomers slowly acquired. Like a giant she could charge through the barriers of red tape and reach a successful resolution to any problem—if she wanted to. But that evening in the *loge* she didn't look powerful to Mme Rogers. While the younger woman knit a sweater, the concierge struggled to do a long strip, forty stitches across, full of holes from dropped stitches. When she came to the end of her yarn, she would rip the piece up and begin again.

"Like Penelope," she explained. "Do you think that perhaps she had bad eyes, made mistakes, and for that reason ripped her work out at night?" Madame Lucie didn't wait for an answer. "Let me ask you a question while we are talking about Monsieur Harton. You know the Americans pretty well. Is he Jewish?"

Madame Rogers couldn't have been more surprised had Mme Lucie asked her if she had a lover on the side. "Why no, his family is Catholic."

"It seems to me he must be Jewish. Why would he name his oldest son Nathan?"

"In the United States people give a child whatever name appeals to them. Besides, their next girl's name is Antoinette and that couldn't be more French."

"Now there's a girl who knows more of the world at eighteen than I ever will. They say she's a waitress at the Place Pigalle, but since the war no one ever knows how a child will turn out." Instead of defending Antoinette, Mme Rogers kept silent. The concierge was now totally distracted from the months beginning with J.

"Right on the Rue Charles d'Alléry, in that building you can see from my window, lived a family of cabinetmakers with a twenty-year-old son, polite as can be. One night, maybe fifteen years ago, they found the body of a young woman—a belly dancer in a Pigalle nightclub. She had been decapitated. The torso was in a suitcase checked at the railroad station. Within a few days the police were swarming all over the neighborhood, and they arrested the boy. He wasn't guillotined though, because the court found him mentally deranged."

The event had shaken the calm of the quiet neighborhood,

although it hadn't been until almost 1970 that things really began to change in cyclonic fashion. Madame Lucie remembered her habit in the postwar days of sitting in a chair in front of her building and sewing while her grandchildren played. From that vantage point she had watched the activity of the sawmill, the garage, the small ironworks across the street. It was the calm of people's working lives. Then all that had been torn down and replaced by the two apartment buildings. The tiny passage was suddenly charged with cars and the noisy disorder of personal lives. Madame Lucie disliked the teenagers—little delinquents she called them—who hung out on the sidewalks, their radios blaring American music, their raucous voices producing new slang words she didn't know but whose meaning she could guess. She professed to be frightened, but her real feelings were something different.

Madame Lucie's reveries were interrupted by a pounding at the door of the *loge*. The old woman asked who it was, to no effect. The banging continued until she shuffled to the other side of the room and released the lock. A large, coarse-looking woman with dyed red hair pushed her way in.

"*Bonsoir*, Mme Lemaire," she shouted in a strange accent.

"Hello, Irène. I could tell it was you from that pounding. You can see I have company." The two guests acknowledged each other.

"I'm sorry to bother you, Mme Lemaire. I'll stop by after I've cleaned for Mme Guido." With that she left as clumsily as she had entered.

"Poor woman, but a very brave one," the concierge commented. Irène was a Polish refugee, orphaned by the war. Having wandered several years in her native land, she had, Mme Lucie believed, lost her senses, and something had happened to her hearing. In Paris, Irène wandered also. She roamed the Faubourg St. Antoine, sometimes stopping to talk with the Africans who cleaned the gutters with their brooms made of twigs.

"She has no place to live. Sometimes she'll take up with an Algerian, the next week it's a black. I think Irène is oversexed." Despite that part of her reputation, everyone in the neighborhood trusted Irène completely. For some artisans she ran errands; a concierge leaving town on vacation or for a few days rest would choose Irène for a replacement. She cleaned apartments, and in the case of Mme Guido was a regular *dame de confiance.*

"What a pair they make," Mme Lucie shook her head. Madame Guido also was often poking her head in the *loge* looking for messages. Always well dressed with a wisp of veil guarding her carefully coiffured dark hair, Mme Guido was one woman whose age was a mystery to the uninitiated.

"If she's less than seventy, then I'm twenty-five," the shriveled old woman smiled. "And an adventuress of the first order. Maman had a saying about women like her: 'Every time she takes off her blouse, it's not just to shout "Vive la République." ' Maman was serious and hardworking, but she knew what was going on."

Madame Lucie wondered how much her mother had known about her own adventures in Caen when she pursued Pierre. She had certainly predicted how badly Aunt Suzanne's marriage might turn out, though she did not live to see Uncle Eugène ruining their lives with his incessant chasing of women. Madame Lucie's aunt had finally arranged a legal separation and didn't hear from her husband for almost a decade, until shortly after the war. Then the news was pathetic. Eugène was dying in a charity hospital in Caen, and Aunt Suzanne rushed like a saint to care for him in his last moments.

"Life is so bitter," Mme Lucie decided.

"Madame Guido looks pretty serious to me, not at all like your uncle."

"Serious? She was serious once, for about three months while her husband was dying. Every day she decked herself out in her finest and visited him. She rose to the occasion. Now she does the same, only it's to seek her fortune in the dance halls on the Rue de Lappe. Imagine what she'll find there!"

Only three blocks from the Passage des Chats, the Rue de Lappe had been called the most dangerous street in Paris by Simenon's Inspector Maigret. There, in Mme Guido's dance halls, Jack of *The Razor's Edge* had reencountered the down-and-out Sophie. For a year or so Mme Rogers had skirted the street and its reputation until, late for work one day, she had taken it as a short cut. Narrower but longer than the Passage, the Rue de Lappe was sleepy in the daytime. This sleepiness seemed a portent of its nighttime dangers, mysteries, and decadence.

"Rue de Lappe dangerous?" Harton had snickered. "Why, at night the tour buses pull up, the Chinese restaurants open their doors, a few hired toughs walk around to create an illusion of adventure. Really—the place is like Disneyland. Passage des Chats is more interesting."

It was true that the Passage offered itself up to the novelist, artist, sociologist, anthropologist, or anyone else wanting an assortment of humanity. Nowhere else did the mailman strut so grandly, the hurdy-gurdy man play not for tourists but for artisans, a baron come to call on his tenants. In the moonlight a criminal had dashed through the streets discarding the contents of a purse until he found its one treasure and discarded the purse too; in broad daylight a respectably dressed woman had stopped to urinate between parked cars. At six one morning all the inhabitants had spilled onto their balconies in bikini underwear or flowered nightgowns to watch a gang of firemen clean a gasoline spill from an automobile, directed by the hunched-up figure of Mme Lucie. And Mme Blanche, the old fortune-teller in the adjoining building, always had a queue of customers waiting to have their palms read.

A stranger might see all these types and offer up some taxonomy, an analysis, or theory of social behavior, but not Mme Lucie. She had to manipulate them, orient newcomers, protect those she liked from the police or other consequences of their follies, guard their keys, and make sure that one and all acknowledged her with tips at the proper moments of the year. She directed a human symphony, kept all actions in harmony and balance, though each of her tenants was playing a solo part.

"I guess we'd better stop our conversation. Irène will be coming back any minute. She needs to talk to me." Madame Lucie was gracious but firm. When anyone needed to consult her, she was adept at removing all obstacles to personal confidences.

"Between the two of us, I know she wants to ask me for money. I'll have to give her a thousand francs." Madame Lucie meant ten francs, but she always spoke in pre-1958-devaluation terms. She went on to explain that for the last week Irène had been broke and hungry, probably, she thought, because of losing money at the races.

"Madame Guido doesn't hesitate to pass on her bad habits. Poor Irène."

This money transaction would be carried on in secret because it involved more than small change. Madame Lucie's own financial affairs were convoluted. She had layers of money arranged according to rank. In the pocket of her bathrobe, housedress, or apron she kept a changepurse. Under the cushion of her chair was one billfold, and tucked deeper, another. Her checkbook wandered to various hiding places in the room. Several people knew the whereabouts of one or more of these caches, but she alone knew all of them.

Once Mme Rogers had stopped by when the old woman was in a flurry of activity shuffling the papers on her table. Magnifying glass in hand, she was trying to sort medical bills and prescriptions from her check stubs and receipts. Enlisting her visitor's help, she explained that Sister Marie-Ste. Geneviève would be arriving soon to fill our her social security forms reimbursing her for medical expenses.

"I need to put away all the check stubs," and pushing papers this way and that, she tried to convince Mme Rogers that although she trusted the sister, she didn't want her to know all the household business.

Madame Lucie had bureaucratized her finances, each section administered by a different person, none of whom knew the total secret. The amount had to be small: her salary from the baron's family was about three hundred francs for four months; her widow's pension was even less. Yet even to administer this required several people. Most initiated into the system was Monsieur Garbaud, an agreeable young man who worked for the post office. Ten years before he had delivered the mail, struck up an acquaintance with the concierge in her prime, and been integrated into her life. Every other week he arrived at five in the morning to wash the three five-story stairways. The same evening he would return to write her checks from the postal account. This was the crowning part of her system, for whenever Mme Lucie needed cash she had but to send a message to Garbaud via one of the mailmen, and it would arrive with the next delivery.

Petty cash was of course taken charge of by Mme Lucie herself and dispensed to those who shopped for her, ran errands, did favors. Irène would have her ten francs and probably pay it back in services. Thierry, who took little messages around and bought bread, could keep the change. Monsieur Garbaud was paid visibly with aperitifs, bottles of wine, and who knew what else. Garbage collectors and mailmen received wine also, and other little presents Mme Lucie might have in turn received for some favor she had done. The system worked so well that the objectively impoverished old woman had been able to loan Colette money to buy her apartment.

"I just gave her a bit—the Métro loaned her the rest at one percent interest. Madame Lucie felt, after all her trials, that Métro workers led the life of kings. She was also disturbed that, at least in Colette's case, they didn't understand the reciprocity of the system. Her granddaughter, she repeated again, couldn't stop to say hello as often as she might. But this was the younger generation. So far the artisans in her building were fairly punctual with their tips, as was the baron's family when the New Year's offering was due.

From time to time Mme Lucie and Mme Perrugia would take up the topic of the baron, repeating the same stories and vying with each other to provide the most information. Having lived in the neighborhood longer, Mme Perugia knew the details of the marriage settlement, in which the baroness had brought the entire passage and some buildings on the Rue de la Roquette as her dowry. Mme Lucie, however, had actually received visits from the lords of the territory, and, she reported, they treated her like a queen.

"Whenever the baroness came, she sat right down and started asking me about the children. She would ask how their jobs were going and where my grandchildren were going to school. It was like having a conversation with one of the neighbors," she said innocently.

Noblesse oblige remained operative, so it seemed, in Maigret country. The baron's family had had much training in that respect, for his mother had been a great crusader in the cause of feudal France, heading a movement early in the century to keep schools from being secularized, organizing mothers to fight the modern world. His grandmother had died in the great charity bazaar fire of 1898, where the women's corpses had been frozen, so the accounts ran, with their arms extended in imitation of the crucified Christ.

One of the most revealing conversations about the baron had started after a visit from Mme Rosa, the voluptuous concierge from the adjoining building. Confident in her manners, polished in appearance, Mme Rosa seemed out of place in a neighborhood where the inhabitants were becoming more foreign-looking and poverty-stricken.

"She used to be what is politely called the baron's 'private secretary.' " Madame Lucie announced this with an air of impartiality, for she and her counterpart next door had just had a small disagreement. A woman of many moods, she could change from being grandmotherly and solicitous to being efficient and worldly-wise. Now she was serving as a character witness against Mme Rosa, and one duty-bound to tell the truth under oath.

"Of course that's why she also owns a large apartment on the Place Voltaire. When she became concierge, you would have thought a duchess were moving in. The downstairs of the *loge* was redecorated, and two rooms were built upstairs for her daughters."

It was true that Mme Rosa had gotten the better position as concierge. Her half of the old barracks had a semidetached guardhouse as its *loge*, as spacious and airy as Mme Lucie's quarters were cramped and dark. She had more tenants and more prestigious ones, like the Lazimi brothers who supplied many Parisian theaters with furniture and props. But for all that, the world of Mme Rosa and the baron remained something of a mystery.

Harton added little more than confirmation of Mme Lucie's report. "Some woman, that Mme Rosa. They say she had a liaison with the old baron. He's dead now." He knew more about the baron's children; the daughter had inherited Mme Lucie's side of the building, the son, Mme Rosa's. When it came time to clean the old barracks, as De Gaulle's government had ordered for all Parisian buildings, the son had to sell some apartments to pay the bill. French law being complicated, he owned the walls of his building, but not the air within.

"Anyway—guess what business he's in these days?"

Madame Rogers thought it might be railroads, banking, or chemicals.

"Wrong!" Harton shouted. "The great aristocrat has a sex-gadget factory along with some Scandinavians." The image hardly fit with that of his great-grandmother burned in the shape of a crucifix.

"And his sister is even crazier. I met her at a swanky party at David's—you know, that rich sculptor. Who should be there but my landlady telling loudly how she would like to have sex under David's glass coffee table while someone defecated on it. Her hobby, she says, is collecting feces in jars. Any artisan in this building is worth twenty of the baron's kids."

Harton was probably right. No matter what the truth about the baron's offspring, there was certainly something vital in the atmosphere of the building. Across the way one could watch men in gray aprons heating solutions and rubbing them on old wood to restore its patina. Others lugged sofas, or racks of handbags tooled in their workrooms. Their competence was attractive, and they were generous in their treatment of the old concierge, whom they tipped, helped, and tolerated in her infirmity. But whenever one romanticized them, Mme Lucie had other ideas. One evening early in July she and the American were sitting and knitting, while the concierge went over the events of the day.

"That scamp Monsieur Corla is up to his old tricks," she reported.

Corla the cabinetmaker had his workshop on the fourth floor of stairway B. Every morning at eight he would huff his way up the three flights of stairs with what looked like an oversized bowling bag dragging behind him. Seventy years old, he uttered his "good mornings" sourly, reluctantly.

Madame Lucie had as much trouble greeting him graciously when he came to ask about the mail. She was convinced that he had killed his first wife.

"Madame Corla died five years ago—right in the workshop," Harton explained. "And that's how I want to go, brush in hand, putting paint on the canvas." Corla's workshop faced Harton's apartment, and the artist happened to be home when it happened. The old cabinetmaker was shouting in the stairwell, so that Harton knew it meant trouble and not just another of Corla's rages at his wife.

A Parisian Concierge

"There she was, lying on the floor, not quite dead. So I told Corla to get an ambulance while I gave her mouth-to-mouth resuscitation. The poor woman died on me. Too bad—she was a regular workhorse and nice as well."

"Work was all she did," Mme Lucie continued the old story in preface to telling the new one. Corla had made her carry coal for the stove, wood for the furniture he was making, all the supplies. She was indeed a workhorse, who did the shopping in between her chores for Corla.

"She went up the stairs twenty times a day even though she had a bad heart. Doctor Mourant told Corla he was killing her—right outside the *loge* one day—and all he got for his trouble was cursing. The doctor was practically foaming at the mouth."

Madame Corla's death had been much regretted in the building; it was a moment Harton at least would never forget. Everyone said kind words to Corla, not because they wanted to comfort him but because they truly missed his wife. In any case, Corla found comfort soon enough on his own. He put an ad in the paper for a girlfriend, and she materialized within a week.

"A nice-looking woman about fifty-five who worked in an office near the Place Voltaire. Eventually they married, but I'm afraid the poor thing didn't know what she was in for."

The relationship had been stormy, as the building knew from seeing one or the other walking off in a huff—more often than not the new Mme Corla. Today had been the coup de grace; Mme Lucie approached the end of her story.

"She banged on my door—I don't know why she chose me, but people stop to tell me their troubles. That's how I know everything. She said not to look for her on the street anymore, to forward her mail, but not to tell Corla the address. She gave me a nice tip and then said that she had just found that old scamp, her husband, in the workshop with Irène."

"Was something bad going on?" Mme Rogers asked.

"I don't know, and anyway she didn't blame Irène. How

[99]

could she? Everyone knows she's disturbed. There's something missing in her head. It's not the same as when Uncle Jacques found Aunt Suzanne—she knew what she was doing. But it's the same kind of situation, if you know what I mean."

"Well, not exactly, but you've always said that your aunt knew a lot about the world," Mme Rogers replied.

"A lot? Why, she knew everything." And Mme Lucie, after a year or more of talking about her family, which had seemed respectably middle-class and as Victorian as any, told the full story of Aunt Suzanne on a Sunday morning in the bakery. Her expression didn't change, but the quality of her memories did from that time on. No longer had the move to Lisieux been one of opportunity; her father, she would say later, had been drinking, her parents were on the verge of divorce. She had always pointed to her responsibilities as concierge; in the future she would occasionally call the job degrading and describe it as somehow emblematic of all that had transpired in her lifetime.

Yet for all that, Mme Lucie had a certain admiration for Aunt Suzanne's getting her soldier, for her own fortitude in pursuing Pierre, of the sense of humor her father had always maintained even in the worst of times. "Imagine the order of the leeks!" Though they functioned badly, her eyes kept their twinkle.

"How complicated life is. And I'm going to tell you something else that may shock you." Madame Lucie had put down her knitting. "Have you noticed anything different about Colette?" she asked.

"Just that she looks more splendid than ever," Mme Rogers responded. In that summer of lavender fashions, Colette wore a white eyelet blouse, a fluttering lavender skirt, the highest of heels as she walked her dog. Her auburn hair hung in ringlets.

"Everyone finds her beautiful, and I'm happy. She and Michel are my favorite grandchildren." Both served her in different ways, Michel with his attention and Colette because she was congruent with Mme Lucie's memories of adventures and derring-do. "But why do you think she's never married?"

That was indeed a riddle, especially for a grandmother whose major adventures had involved secret conquests first of Philippe and then of Pierre.

"For the last year or so Colette has harangued us about marriage, saying that she would never think of it." Madame Lucie, who was not bad at sensing secret meanings behind loud protestations, had at first been puzzled. Colette had seemed the romantic type. Sensing an affinity of dauntless spirits, Mme Lucie had given her grandaughter Philippe's ring on her eighteenth birthday. Colette had appeared moved then by its meaning—the high adventure of young love and the high tragedy of its end. Later Antoine's amorous intrigues and the perils they involved came to fascinate her. So Colette's months of denunciation for what appeared the culmination of her ancestors' romantic natures, of their youthful quests, did seem incongruous. Then she proved that she was indeed one of them.

"Now Colette's announced that she's pregnant and is going to keep the baby," Mme Lucie reported. The family was in an uproar, except for the old woman, who in the final analysis wasn't surprised at all:

"She was always a headstrong rebel."

5

Family Time

Paris, 1978

As Mme Lucie passed into her eighties, one slender ritual held her to her family. Too feeble, so she said, to visit them on Sunday, too sick to eat their food, she stayed in the *loge* and silently demanded that they make the contacts. Antoine alone did. Every evening he stepped off the six o'clock train from the suburbs, where he worked on a government crew repairing machines. Reversing his early morning circuit, he walked from the Gare de Lyon to the Passage des Chats, a satchel in tow, a certain weariness on his face. Although close to sixty, he still looked vigorous and fit, and the several kilometers he covered at both ends of his journey gave him a ruddy complexion. Colette's toddling son, he said, kept him young, too, with the squeals of welcome every night and the tussles on the floor. Before that pleasure, however, even before seeing Mariette, he stopped at the *loge*.

Antoine always rapped at the door and entered without waiting for a response. Briskly he kissed Mme Lucie's withered cheeks while she rolled up her knitting.

"Everything fine, Maman?" And as she went through the

litany of her aches and discomforts, intestines and rheumatism, he fixed himself a Pernod.

"You know, Maman, it's not much fun visiting you when all I hear are complaints. A man who has worked all day needs a smiling face and a little comfort himself." Madame Lucie sat stone-faced as Antoine continued with a comparison between his mother and Mariette. His wife had more problems than most women—a tumor that was now the size of a lemon and needed an operation, and a grandchild to care for while Colette worked. Yet Mariette, he said, always greeted him with a smile.

Madame Lucie was interested enough to discuss Mariette's tumor for a while. Then, satisfied with his visit, Antoine went home.

Madame Lucie, too, was always satisfied that the visits had occurred, even though they usually left her grumbling.

"My children have no idea what it is to be old and still hard at work. If Mariette had to lead my life, she wouldn't be so pleasant," she said to Mme Rogers later that evening. Mariette often bore the burden of Mme Lucie's criticism. Yet she had been the much-desired bride who had ended Antoine's perilous escapades.

"We told him," Mme Lucie recounted, "marry a Turk, marry a Negress—but don't return without a wife." So Antoine had returned with a North African wife of Spanish descent. But despite an acceptable physiognomy, she had been more than the Lemaire parents had bargained for. Mariette couldn't read, couldn't cook, sew, or knit! A perfectly unaccomplished bride, perfectly, in Mme Lucie's words, "uncivilized."

Antoine and Mariette had returned to a warm welcome, but they needed more. In the housing shortage that raged in Paris, the only place to live was the *loge*. Soon Colette came along, which meant five people in one room. While Antoine went off to work and her husband took on odd jobs, Mme Lucie had to take care of her responsibilities and civilize Mariette.

"Her mother, being Spanish, thought work undignified."

Not that they were rich or had servants. In fact, Mariette's mother had worked as a cigar maker for a while, rolling the finished cigars on her thigh to pack them. But when she'd finally had enough of such degradation, she retired to her sofa and let everything fall apart around her.

The indictment of Mariette really began with her mother, whose neglect Mme Lucie had had to remedy—and not under the best of conditions. It was hard to imagine the scene. All of them and a baby in the *loge*, while Mme Lucie not only had her job as concierge, but other work as well. The upholsterers in the building gave her sewing to do.

"Do you know about upholstering?" she asked Mme Rogers. "This tiny space would be filled with yards of fabric, let's say to make drapes and bedcovers to match the other furniture. We would have to navigate around all of it. Besides that I would have to try to find food, and believe me, I didn't hesitate to use the black market, what with a baby and the appetite of two grown men. And if all of that weren't bad enough, the Free French, rude as can be, were guarding the streets. They thought that all other people were traitors; so we'd get a bump here and a push there while going to market. Do you think they taught us anything good by trying Pétain and shooting the others?" These years of discontent returned to their focus on Mariette.

"In the midst of everything I had to take her in hand, teach her to cook, to mend her own clothes, to take care of the baby. Then Pierre would come home to find me still sewing late into the night. '*Ma petite cocotte*'—he always called me that, but not disrespectfully—or 'my poor little wife' and he would rub my neck and shoulders, 'don't work so hard.' And now that he's gone, do you think Mariette will stop for a minute for a little chat?"

Her discontent boiled that evening after Antoine's comparison, after his praise for Mariette's happy smiles.

"She always says that she'll drop by to do my laundry. I am

still waiting for that day to come. If I ask her to do a little errand, she has her house to clean or the baby to take care of. Do you know, Madame," the concierge now looked pitifully at her visitor, "that you and almost anyone else in this building do more for me than my own family?"

Madame Lucie made everyone feel her children's desertion. While she then praised her neighbors to Antoine, his only response took the form of counterpraise for his wife. Or he tried to convince his mother that she was not so infirm as she thought. The tangle was choking them all, so Mme Rogers tried to change the subject by asking how the baby was. Usually Mme Lucie could rise to the occasion by talking about his antics and finding resemblances between the little Louis and his grandfather. But not tonight.

"Now that the baby is here, Mariette uses him as an excuse for everything."

In fact Colette's pregnancy had turned out to be a grand event, deliberately so. After a few weeks of trying to dissuade her and counseling abortion, the family adopted Colette's own pride and defiance as if in concert. The women began ostentatiously knitting. Antoine wheeled home a shiny pram. An inauguration, a national holiday seemed in the offing. And when the great moment came and went in a fairly regular fashion, the neighbors recognized that for all their expectations a baby was a baby.

Still, Colette maintained her flair, smartly conducting the pram down the littered passage, avoiding animals and offal nonchalantly. As she passed, the young workers stared, not because of the baby but because of Colette.

"Look at her, look at her grandmother—what women!" Even Harton's refrain remained constant. "She wanted the baby, and she got the baby. Without the complication of a man around the house. I've always said those Lemaire women know how to get what they want." It was hard not to think, if one knew the story, of Mme Lucie chasing Pierre to the garrison at Caen.

But while Harton thought that Colette believed the father incidental, the concierge's version was somewhat different.

"Of course she wanted the baby, but I think she'd like the father, too." One had trouble figuring out the real story from Mme Lucie's reports not just of Colette's situation but of her own and her mother's as well.

"Today," Mme Lucie began, "women can do just as they please—have a baby or not—without much trouble. When my mother was thirty-nine or so, she lost great quantities of blood and I had to care for her. Only after my first child was born did I find out that she had aborted. One was modest in those days." Madame Lucie believed that men, her own husband included, would keep women perpetually pregnant. In her case, she had had to say no to more children, although at other times she gave Pierre credit for limiting their family.

As for Colette, Mme Lucie insisted that she had "wanted" the baby.

"Of course she wanted the baby. Now women don't have to have them, don't have always to worry about being pregnant as I was. Colette refused an abortion no matter how much Antoine and Mariette pressured her." Whatever Colette decided, Mme Lucie maintained that the legalization of abortion in 1974 was the greatest blessing women had received in her memory.

Madame Rogers remembered the abortion victory well, for she had watched the debate with Mme Lucie before the old woman had decided that television was nothing but noise. Alternately knitting and then putting her work down, Mme Lucie had much to say about the debates.

"Look at those old men!" she mocked. "What do they know about babies? What do they know about anything?" And when the bill had passed, she was triumphant. "I've always said that if men had to bear a child for every one his wife did, no family would have more than two." Then she proceeded to applaud Mme Veil, the minister who had pushed the bill through. The situation—a Catholic woman cheering abortion—was jarring. In retrospect it made one wonder why Colette had vetoed the idea so completely.

"Maybe they'll get together after all," Mme Rogers suggested. She had seen Jean-Claude, the baby's father, pushing the pram with Colette, and sometimes, she knew from Mme Lucie, they took him on outings when the day was fair. How dapper and smart they looked, the handsome father smiling at his son and solicitous after the porcelain-beautied mother. Only one thing clouded the scene: Jean-Claude had a wife and a twelve-year-old daughter living a few blocks away.

The story came out only later. The two had met in the Métro, where Colette was head of the station. Gone was the old Métro of faded blue and white tiles, blue-suited women sitting on rickety chairs punching tickets. The new Métro was made for Colette. The modern glass control booth framed her beauty, while the flamboyant orange tiles were, it now seemed in retrospect, an echo of her passionate nature.

"*L'amour*, that's all anyone has in mind down there," Mme Lucie summed it up. "There's nothing to do. I can't tell you how many sweaters Colette has knit while she's supposed to be working. No wonder there's so much hanky-panky going on."

At other times Mme Lucie was proud of her granddaughter and listed her responsibilities. "It's no job for a woman, I assure you. Colette has charge of the money, has to close up at night. Men insult her, and you remember how she was attacked last year."

Colette had been attacked, and more than once. Each time, after the vacation that was normally granted for recuperation from such an incident, she returned to work. For as Mme Lucie pointed out, sometimes with pride, at others with scorn, Colette "earned a good living."

During the past few years it was less the money than Jean-Claude who bound Colette to her job. Driving the trains through underground Paris, he was the closest Colette could come to meeting an adventurer. The Passage des Chats hadn't much to offer in that regard—only a series of artisans' apprentices with whom she had grown up. Even the biggest excitement in the neighborhood—the resurfacing and cleaning of the two ancient buildings—had left her cold. The gangs of new men were just more familiar artisanal faces.

"They leered at her and pumped me for information about my granddaughter. Men have little on their minds but that," Mme Lucie said. "When it came to doing the windows around her apartment, the workers fought to be on that particular crew." As for Colette, it turned out, she left town.

Colette's neighborhood chastity did nothing to stop rumors that had circulated since she came of age. The snooty Mme Bernard had her linked with successive printer's apprentices, while Mme Rosa, the concierge next door, whispered that she was sleeping with the wallpaper hanger who lived on the floor above.

"Imagine it. Everyone connected her with Monsieur Paul and him with four children! But then, most of them have watched her grow up and expect anything." Madame Lucie proceeded to list the defects of character that accompanied Colette's beauty: she was headstrong, temperamental, used to having her own way or at least used to demanding it. As she continued her analysis, the old woman lifted herself from the chair and toddled to the armoire where she kept what she called her "archives." The cupboard overflowed with bundles, folded clothing, shoeboxes, a Protestant Bible, a few stacks of papers, letters bound with string. From the bottom shelf she pulled out one of the shoeboxes, the one filled with photographs. This was the one item Mme Lucie always pulled out for her American visitor, and Mme Rogers wondered each time why it was so hidden at the bottom.

"Here are their first communion pictures," she said, squinting and sizing each up with her hand to determine if they were indeed the right photos. Colette and her sister, Simone, were frozen, looking at heaven in their respective pious poses. Madame Rogers had seen them before and hoped she would see others. She loved the photos of Mme Lucie and Pierre on their vacations on the Riviera. In her fifties then, the concierge had been robust, laughing, and her husband held her close to him. It was a twin to a picture on the nightstand—the one Mme Lucie kissed every night before she went to sleep.

"This is the one I'm looking for," and as she passed it, Mme Rogers could see Pierre, Colette, and Philippe's oldest son, Michel, on the beach at Bernières.

"That's it, it was taken near Trouville, my first trip back to Caen after the British had bombed it to bits." Madame Lucie hated the British for destroying Caen, and she had come to hate them more when she had visited on her vacation, only to find all the old landmarks gone, Grand-mère's bakery, all the old fortifications and garrison buildings, churches in rubble. But her parent's house on the Rue Le Bras still stood.

"And, at least the beaches were there, but even they had changed. I took some needlework to sit by the ocean. And what did I find? The women were lying on the sand—asleep—half-naked."

Madame Rogers agreed that sunbathing was boring. "It also gives me a headache."

"Exactly. Besides, you never know what will turn up when you take a little work with you. I supported my Philippe and myself when he had to get out of the city for his lungs." And she told the story of an earlier return to Normandy, of summers near St. Pars les Vaud when she did needlework and the boys helped the farmers in return for food and firewood.

"The summers when we went to Menton on the Riviera, I was always ready to work. Our room had a hot plate so I could fix coffee in the morning; at night we would lie in bed watching the car lights as they crossed the border into France—it was so peaceful."

From Menton they had visited Monte Carlo for a day. It was

another world to Mme Lucie, the croupiers who could only wear pocketless clothing, the rich or struggling who sometimes had to make a visit to their "aunt"—meaning the closest pawnshop. Prince Rainier, Mme Lucie explained, had married Grace Kelly for her money when his real love was Micheline Prel, the actress who hadn't a sou. For all the excitement of Monaco, however, Mme Lucie preferred Menton, where she could sit on the beach with one project or another, and watch the fashion parade at her own pace.

"Once I bought some multicolored yarn shot with gold thread to make a shawl. The woman in the *mercerie* loved it so much that she bought it from me to sell, and then gave me more yarn free." The shawl was draped over the back of Mme Lucie's chair now, unused except for remembering.

She often went to her "archives" to find a piece of handiwork that fit her story: the blue silk dress made for her oldest grandson's wedding, a black sweater with gold flecks knit reluctantly after her husband had died, an unfinished mauve ensemble, never stitched together.

"I decided that I wasn't going to go out visiting anymore—so why bother putting it together." It remained in pieces in the armoire.

"But I started to tell you about Colette in Normandy. Then you'll see what we're up against. Every night she wanted to be out, walking, going to the carnival. She was a real adventuress."

"It reminds me, Madame, of your love of adventure in all those stories you told," the American said.

"Do you think so?" she smiled, almost flirtatiously, for a minute, then changed her mind. "But look at me. I'm happy in my *loge*. Once a year Mariette takes me to the eye doctor in the Faubourg St. Germain. Other than that I go nowhere. I've never been to the Eiffel Tower—most Parisians haven't, you know. No, Colette is quite different." One night on that vacation Pierre had told her to spend the evening at home.

Family Time

Failing to change his mind with arguments and tears, she lifted her chin and just walked out the door. Headstrong Colette had stayed out for several hours, until her cousin finally dragged her back howling.

"Michel worshiped her. Even when she was tiny, he would cuddle her, take her for walks, talk baby talk to her. Only this time, he was so infuriated at her for disobeying her grandfather that he slapped her face. He worshiped his grandfather more than he did Colette."

Madame Lucie alternately worried about Colette or was angry with her, just as she swung between pride in her responsible job and thinking that the Métro was a den of vice. Always her grandmother's favorite, Colette began failing in filial duties, her visits becoming less and less frequent after the baby was born. The concierge knew her steps passing the *loge* just as she knew everyone else's. Colette's terrier made it even more apparent that the young woman was passing by without so much as "a little *bonjour*."

"When she needs something she's friendly enough. I saw her every day while she was gathering money together to buy her apartment." It was fine to be a free spirit if filial piety remained intact.

Often it seemed that Mme Lucie chanted her anger in order to exorcise evil spirits. In June and July she chanted her sorrow, at New Year's her gratitude to the artisans for their generosity (unless someone had been stingy). She rehearsed stories of Marie-Louise and the filth of the cats, of Monsieur Corla's killing his wife, of Irène's craziness. But in the evenings, after Antoine's visits, the litany had a family focus. As often as not Mme Rogers would arrive at about seven to find the concierge's chin set or, alternately, a resigned expression in her eyes, which were fixed in an unseeing stare.

Always when in a mood Mme Lucie was impeccably polite, never going immediately to her troubles. Instead she would ask her visitor how her day had been, how the children were, what she had had for dinner or lunch. Soon, her own troubles would have been hanging too long.

"How do you find me?" It was a sign that she should not be found doing too well.

"Why, I was just about to mention that you look tired." With that sanction, Mme Lucie launched into the real matter at hand.

"Mariette's not speaking to Antoine and he's not speaking to me. But I don't care, they're not going to run my life." This was said with determination.

Sometimes Mme Lucie would allude to a particular malaise, letting the matter go for a few days until a torrent of troubles poured forth. Before that she teased and was sadly coquettish, almost begging for questions to answer only vaguely. But tonight, having said the worst, Mme Lucie was ready to tell the story, so much did her son's condemnation bother her.

"Antoine said some very cruel things to me and I don't think I can ever forgive him. He even mentioned you." At this, Mme Rogers's heart sank. Having listened to family stories for years, she was culpable even though she never asked questions. Had Antoine, she wondered, overheard their conversations, especially Mme Lucie's public criticisms of Mariette?

"Do you remember last week when the concierge from around the corner visited?" Madame Rogers remembered those several afternoons well, for Mme Courrier was a new face to her. A hearty woman who looked younger than her sixty years, Mme Courrier has breezed into the *loge*, listened politely while Mme Lucie introduced her American visitor, and then settled down for a good talk. Madame Rogers had sought to extricate herself once the concierge had other companionship so that she could take care of her own household affairs. But Mme Lucie insisted that she remain. Then, the two old friends proceeded to talk about everything and everyone as if no one else had been present. The talk was so animated that Kiki the canary chirped louder and faster than usual.

Antoine, too, had entered for his own visit, and when that happened, Mme Rogers had been able to leave without protests from anyone.

"Well, after you left Antoine and Mme Courrier both stayed for more than an hour. The same thing happened the next day, only you didn't visit that afternoon."

A simple encounter in the *loge* was the cause of the family quarrel, for Mme Courrier was a woman with a past.

"She looks good for her age," Mme Lucie explained, "but twenty years ago and more, she was the neighborhood beauty." Taking up the standard, both Antoine and Pierre frankly admired her, stood occasionally under the archway to get the full benefit of her comings and goings. While Mme Lucie had taken their preoccupation calmly, Mariette's jealousy flared. For Mme Courrier was not an innocent; she had borne an illegitimate child.

"It was a deception in love. Madame Courrier—I call her Madame though she never married—thought the man in question would marry her, but the minute she became pregnant he said his farewell." Madame Lucie went on to explain that Mme Courrier had kept the baby, who had since become a very respectable man.

"The neighborhood women, however, were not amused. They chained their husbands to them, and some, like Mariette, became hysterical at the mention of her name." So the situation was nothing new, except that it was thirty years later and Mme Lucie was now seen as complicit.

"She practically accused me of being a panderer, and Antoine carried the message. Of course, I don't blame him entirely. After being forced to sleep on the floor, he isn't in the best of moods." Madame Lucie had little good to say about women who ranted at their husbands. Having seen jealousy close up in her Aunt Suzanne and Mariette, she condemned it as pernicious. Mariette, she thought, was turning a good thing sour.

"Look at my son. He doesn't smoke, doesn't drink, pays me a visit every night, and then goes home to his wife. Antoine is serious." Every long weekend Antoine drove a hundred kilometers north of Paris, where he had purchased a run-down farmhouse. Not resting, he had completely restored it, planted a rose garden and a plot for vegetables. When he retired he wanted to retire there, away from the city.

"So you can see, he's not one for intrigue. And what is Mariette's response to all this? She invents problems and now says that she would rather divorce Antoine than move to the country." Madame Lucie began to recount her daughter-in-law's imbroglios with the people of Picardy. They were cold, according to Mariette, so she wouldn't buy any food there, preferring to cart all their supplies from Paris where goods were more expensive. She had no use for the other Parisians, who like the younger Lemaires, were buying old houses flooding the market as small farms were absorbed into larger holdings.

Mariette was a woman at odds with the world. Her scrapes and quarrels were legendary in the neighborhood. Immaculate in her dress and housekeeping after a slovenly childhood, she ranted at the old fortune-teller in her building for having a dirty doormat. Mothers who let their children play loose in the courtyard heard from her. For a while Mariette had worked illegally for leather pocketbook manufacturers in the building—a couple of francs an hour, nothing reported to the government—but she soon broke with them and had forced her mother-in-law, their concierge, to do likewise.

"Now she wants me to call Mme Courrier and tell her not to visit. If Mariette spent any time here, I might consider doing it. But she wants me to be alone, turning away people who are nice enough to give me a little companionship."

Madame Rogers was hard-pressed not to comment. But from having witnessed the quarrels for a while, she knew that silence was the wisest course. Any taking of sides would be reported back immediately, used as arguments for one side or the other. Besides, Mme Lucie had mentioned that she was somehow involved.

"They gave me this alternative. Instead of telling her not to visit at all, I can tell her that should Antoine arrive, she must leave at once, the way you do."

So there it was. Madame Rogers could see that no way existed not to be used in the family argument. Having pre-empted other strategies, Antoine and Mariette kept their silence, but so did Mme Lucie. She set her chin and suffered Antoine's absence for more than a week before the visits resumed. Some kind of compromise had been reached, but of what nature no one knew. Except that Mme Courrier stopped visiting her neighbor in the Passage des Chats.

As far as anyone could tell, it was the birth of Colette's baby that had caused Mariette's nerves, already stretched tight, to snap, it seemed, for good. In fact, the dismissal of Mme Courrier was only a dull replay of the termination, after more than thirty years, of Doctor Mourant's services. It all began when that old dandy arrived late for the delivery. But because the baby was beautiful, fat-cheeked, and looking more than anything like his grandfather, Doctor Mourant's sins were temporarily forgotten. Soon after, however, Colette, weakened by the drama surrounding the event, fell victim to an infection and couldn't nurse her son. Her temperature rising, her breasts aching, she could do nothing but sob.

"I'm going to die. My son will be an orphan," she moaned, thinking as well of Jean-Claude, who couldn't be relied on.

With that Mariette had picked up the phone and ordered Doctor Mourant, who had brought Colette into this world, to hurry over and keep her from leaving it. To his discredit, he refused.

"I have a *real* emergency to tend. Bind her breasts and give her some aspirin." And with that, he quit their lives forever. Mariette never forgave him. Nor could anyone else in the family.

Madame Lucie put the best face on a bad situation.

"Now we all use Doctor Posta—a Moroccan, I think. He's here to help whenever we need him. Besides, I always disliked Doctor Mourant's wife." Madame Mourant had committed a few sins herself. As head of the animal protection society, she gave Marie-Louise food for her cats. Whenever Mme Lucie complained about the messes the cats were making in the building, Marie-Louise threatened to send Mme Mourant around for an inspection.

"Maybe that's what she meant by putting a curse on me."

Fortunately for Mme Lucie's own nerves, Antoine's other daughter lived outside Paris, about thirty miles away in a town where her husband was postman. Away from the storm center, Simone was not completely forgotten, nor was her husband, about whom the old woman had definite ideas. He was a smoker, three and four packs a day of vile-smelling Gauloises. The fumes upsetting her ideas about proper housekeeping, Simone had once succeeded in making him quit.

"For about a week he didn't smoke, but he doesn't have the force of character to keep a promise."

Like her husband, Simone too fell short in Mme Lucie's opinion. She couldn't point to anything specific, but Colette remained her favorite, despite—or maybe because of—her adventures.

"Simone's like Mariette, a fanatical housekeeper. She scrubs and polishes the entire day. Her children are no easy matter either: one wants to be an archeologist, the other an airline stewardess." With such ambitions Simone's children couldn't leave school at a young age, but instead would have to achieve, working diligently on their studies. At home they couldn't be asked to lift a finger. Madame Lucie was proud of their accomplishments, but complained on Simone's behalf of the extra work.

"Then at night, after all that, she's supposed to entertain

her husband, if you know what I mean. Between us, he's a fanatic, always wanting her to play. That doesn't make him any different from most men, who can think only about such things. A woman, of course, after she's had a child or two, has other things on her mind. But husbands have no understanding of what women have to do.

"We have a saying in France that a woman is more wife than mother or vice versa. Well, Simone is more mother than wife." The two qualities, according to Mme Lucie, were almost incompatible. A few weekends before, when visiting her parents' country home, Simone had rushed to sleep with her mother, so much did her husband's desire upset her. Their bedroom incompatibility was obviously the topic of much discussion. Colette, however, was a different story.

"Now Colette is much more womanly, much more sexual. It embarrasses me sometimes to think of all the men who have shared her bed." As concierge, Mme Lucie knew as much about who entered her granddaughter's apartment and how long they stayed as she did about any other tenant. Strangely, she talked more about the former and less about the latter.

"Sometimes I think of Aunt Suzanne and all she knew at a young age. But even she settled down after her children were born. Uncle Eugène continued, like all men."

Periods of peace could establish themselves for the Lemaires in the Passage des Chats. At those times Madame diverted herself with the radio. She especially loved "Les Grosses Têtes," a question-and-answer show featuring prominent intellectuals and others renowned for their cleverness. Always tucking away the most amusing problems, she would spring them on visitors. Max Meunier, the all-night radio announcer, also kept her company, so she said with a grin, on nights when she couldn't sleep.

"He's very good to people, especially truckers. Imagine this. A while ago two sets of twins were born to truckers who were on the road. Max Meunier announced it, so they would have the good news immediately. So if you need an urgent message sent, just call him."

Madame Lucie also liked vocalists, because she had always loved singing.

"Pierre Pierret is a bit daring, but so much fun that he's good for all of us. I like Jacques Brel, except that his 'Port d'Amsterdam' is off-color." Brel, Mme Lucie explained, owned property in Tahiti, like Gauguin the painter.

"I always wondered whether he was related to the Monsieur Gauguin who lived across the street from us in Caen, right on the spot where the Caisse d'Epargne was built."

This Gauguin had bought the property from two elderly brothers, who had made the strings for musical instruments from catgut and had given Mme Lucie's mother the solid silver goblets and table settings that had formed part of Mme Lucie's own dowry. Their successor, Gauguin, was a locksmith whose brother served as conductor on presidential trains. Once he had shaken hands with a President of the Republic—Mme Lucie forgot which—and releasing his grip found a hundred francs in the palm of his hand. The Caisse d'Epargne and the rats that followed, Lami's decoration of their balcony—such were Mme Lucie's thoughts in those moments of familial tranquility.

Then too, Mariette would care uncomplainingly for the little boy in Colette's former apartment, which she had surrendered to her parents in exchange for childcare. She took up residence in and paid the rent on her parents' one-room flat. Daily she went to the Métro and enjoyed what time Jean-Claude could spare from his other family. Antoine came for his aperitif each night, occasionally persuading Mariette to bring the baby around to be hugged by his *Mémère*. That he looked like her family pleased her—the child was adorable, very advanced, and, like Mme Lucie's own father, full of fun and childish pranks. He also, and here she found much fault, had plastic soldiers, an American revolver, and other toy instruments of war. What was the world coming to, she thought, when war was virtually forced upon children.

In the meantime, too, the artisanal world continued to feel a kind of change that left Mme Lucie at a loss. Though the same cycles persisted, she couldn't understand the decline of the cabinetmakers and their replacement by tenants of a different stripe. First, the artists had flooded in, four or five being a flood when one is speaking of artists. Foreigners for the most part, they caused Mme Lucie very little difficulty: they were strangers, their work was strange, and so their manners would be also. A woman like Sondra from California (where savages lived), who did sculpture in plastic, would naturally wear old peajackets and gypsy skirts and lead a strange life. At least she did something comprehensible, with her hands, out of palpable material.

More distressing were the new kinds of French men and women who were in things like planning, informational services, and the like. What did they do? Mme Lucie used to wonder out loud. Where was their equipment, their goods and materials? In any case, she never had to wonder too long, for they were a transient crew. But even the older artisans were changing their ways, like Monsieur Sabre, who at least four times a year went to Lebanon and other Near Eastern countries to upholster. Didn't, she thought, they know how to upholster in those places? It was, after all, not a difficult skill to acquire. What disturbed her more was the obvious change in Sabre's character and way of life. Frankly, he was getting a swelled head, his clothes became smarter, his wife (who kept the books) more demanding, and together they began talking about sending their children to the United States to school or at least for a holiday.

From time to time Philippe and his family, far off in a town near Le Havre where he worked for Renault, crossed Mme

Lucie's mind. Philippe, never a problem like Antoine, Colette, Mariette, and Simone, had with Nanette raised four children, all of whom seemed more or less insubstantial to her now, living so far away and hardly ever coming to visit. Their oldest boy, the wartime baby, Michel, with whom Mme Lucie had fled the initial phase of liberation, was an exception. From Créteil in the suburbs he called her regularly, while he and his wife visited once a month or so for dinner.

These dinners caused a flurry of preparation. The day before Mme Lucie would put her thinning hair into curlers and face the world in that state all the next day.

Seeing her that way, Mme Rogers would ask what cavalier was paying a call, and Mme Lucie would announce Michel's impending arrival. Too polite to ask someone not to visit, she let curlers serve the purpose.

She also worried about food, even though Michel usually brought everything necessary.

"I bought sardines without bones for an hors d'oeuvre. Michel says he'll bring the rest. But between the two of us, I've had Mme Perrugia buy me some extra supplies." She always traced the source of this anxiety to the first meal she had cooked for her husband—a seamstress's meal, she called it.

Madame Rogers knew that the old woman worried about food. Going to get Mme Lucie a biscuit from the cupboard during her sickness, she had found what seemed a year's supply of sardines, boxes of sugar and powdered milk, bags of macaroni, and canned vegetables. Having heard many of Mme Lucie's stories, she decided that deprivation for much of her adult life and the precariousness of her access to supplies in old age had stocked the larder as much as had the memories of her husband's appetite.

While they canceled one night's visit, the pink curlers demanded a call the following day for a report. Madame Lucie was always eager to reiterate Michel's success, a fact evident, for one thing, in his owning two cars. He worked for one of those companies whose functioning and production was such a mystery to his grandmother. In his case, she hardly thought about it, for Michel was dutiful, and an evening with him gave her so much pleasure. The name Michel, Mme Rogers discovered on her own, has associations with resistance and comfort in times of distress. Hence its popularity in wartime, though Mme Lucie would never have acknowledged such connections with the Free French or other resistants. Instead Michel was her personal treasure. Because he could do no wrong, he immunized his entire family from criticism. Philippe, whose picture showed a fat and happy man, was about to retire from the Renault factory. His dream was to find himself a little country house near St. Pars les Vaud, where he had found refuge from his adolescent frailty. His retirement would be a grand event, the company providing a celebratory dinner for seven hundred of Philippe's co-workers. Madame Lucie worried only that Nanette might fail in living on a pension.

"That woman, good as she is, can't keep to a budget. She's raised four children and even her grandchildren without a murmur of complaint. But I wish she were more like Mariette when it comes to money."

Except for that, Mme Lucie never got upset with her eldest son's family, even though the three daughters had married young and foolishly, and dropped their children off for Nanette to raise. One had even deserted both husband and child for another man. Yet how little it all mattered to the old woman, their grandmother. It was different with Colette.

As the perilous J months approach, Mme Rogers feared a crisis of some kind. But a change had occurred in Mme Lucie's life to distract her, if only temporarily. She had had a telephone installed, and most people were surprised that it arrived without advance warning.

"I called one week to ask for it, and a few weeks later, there it was," she announced proudly. Madame Lucie did not have to explain further. Most people had to wait a year or more for a Parisian phone, but she had influence of a kind not expected in someone so poor, so objectively inconsequential to the larger world.

"It's wonderful. Whenever I need company, I don't have to sit here helplessly anymore. I just give Mme Perrugia a little call. I've called Mariette, Doctor Posta, and even Sister Marie-Ste. Geneviève." Madame Rogers began receiving calls whenever Mme Lucie wanted her at hours other than the official one for visits. And Mariette could not escape a few words with her mother-in-law. As the months passed and the calls continued, however, she stopped answering the phone.

"I know she's there," Mme Lucie would grumble. "Colette just took the baby over." It was like the arrival of the first television set in a family, which always resulted in an orgy of viewing. Except, with the phone, outsiders were drawn into the new gadget's use whether they wanted to be or not.

Madame Lucie had another secret connected with the telephone, one she guarded closely until the right moment.

"Come see what the telephone people brought me today," she coyly invited Mme Rogers as she passed the *loge* one afternoon. The half-door had been opened, and Mme Lucie sat facing it, all attention given to sensing the owner of the footsteps she heard. The red oilcloth that covered her table had been cleared of its usual papers, knitting, and dishes. Alone, in the middle, was a telephone book, not the huge two-volume *Bottin* but a smaller manual about as fat as the directory for a medium-size American city.

"It's a manual for telephone services. See if you find anything familiar."

Madame Rogers had already spotted the familiar object. Below the title of the manual was a colored photo of Mme Lucie using her telephone.

"Why do you think they picked an old woman like me?" she

asked rhetorically. "Probably they needed my glamour to make the telephone look better." For all the fun she poked at herself, the directory became her pride and joy, prominently displayed for a while, then pulled out when a visitor arrived who hadn't seen the precious cover.

But before the telephone was a year old, it became a cursed object. One day a woman called asking for Mlle Colette Lemaire. As cautious with callers as she was with strangers knocking at the door of her *loge*, Mme Lucie found out the name of the caller and the purpose of her inquiry before volunteering any information. Then:

"No, there's no one by that name in my building."

Hobbling up the three flights of stairs, she banged at her granddaughter's door so loudly that a dead person would have been startled. In fact, Colette, working nights that week, had been sleeping and angrily asked what the old woman thought she was doing disturbing her like that.

"Well, I didn't kill myself climbing these stairs merely to say *bonjour*. Jean-Claude's wife just called me. She's found out everything."

Madame Lucie yelled her message through the closed door not merely for Colette's benefit, but so that Jean-Claude could hear were he there.

"What a disagreeable disposition Colette is getting," she commented later. "I go to help her and she can't even say thank you." But even more disagreeable were the daily calls from Mme Jean-Claude insisting that she had good information that Mlle Colette was indeed in that apartment. Then one day the calls stopped.

That evening Mme Rogers found the concierge dejected, staring into space as she did whenever some trouble had overwhelmed her.

"My savior!" she sighed to her guest. Without asking how Mme Rogers's day had been, she launched into her story.

"Madame Jean-Claude somehow found Colette's apartment. It was a regular cat fight." Madame Lucie explained that the argument could be heard throughout the building. She felt disgrace for the whole family, something akin to what Uncle Jacques had felt upon finding Aunt Suzanne that Sunday morning in the bakery.

This encounter proved more than a disgrace. From that moment Colette's adventure turned to dust, her adventurer to clay. Jean-Claude had received an ultimatum from his wife and began cutting back his visits to the Passage des Chats. Colette, for her part, could not understand a hero without conviction and courage, who toed the mark for a drab little housewife and a dull-witted (so she supposed) teenager. He was turning down glamour and excitement in favor of mediocrity, and finally she told him so. Jean-Claude became violent that evening and made his exit permanently.

"How life is bitter, how it changes," the concierge told Mme Rogers after seeing the swollen, purplish face of her granddaughter. Colette took a week-long medical leave from the Métro.

By the time July came, Mme Lucie had developed what she called a "spider" in her head—a cluster of bad ideas that gripped her with multiple appendages. Antoine, Mariette, Colette, and the baby had gone to Picardy for their vacation. From there Colette would go to Corsica with a new young man she knew—an engineer, Mme Lucie mustered enough strength to announce. In their absence she envisioned all sorts of calamities, including mortal illness.

"Doctor Posta will be going on vacation and so will the pharmacist. Then what will become of me?" The butcher who sent over a beefsteak every noon was closing too. Her list grew longer, swelling like a leech gorging on its host. The only comfort she found was in the thought that the baron's family woule be sending over a little extra money because she herself stayed on the job.

That, however, led to reminiscing about the vacations she had always taken with her dear husband.

"If I weren't so afraid of dying, I'd wish I were in the ground next to him."

"Did you always go to Menton?" Mme Rogers asked, searching for some subject that could bring the two of them out of their gloom.

"Did you always go to Menton for vacations?" she repeated.

"Mostly there, but one year we went to Lourdes. I'll never forget it. It's impossible to, even for unbelievers. Have you ever seen it?"

The closest Mme Rogers had ever been to Lourdes was seeing a hospital train bound for the shrine. Waiting at a country station to return to Paris, she had wondered at all the ambulances, at the wheelchaired and maimed people who crowded the quays. Then the train from Lourdes had pulled in, twenty cars long it seemed and filled with more doctors, nurses, and lay attendants than afflicted people. While the train traveled in and out of the station at normal speed and with a normal amount of noise, the pace aboard was slow-motioned, gentle, and otherworldly.

"It was 1951 and Pierre was out of work. After we had been in Lourdes nine days, he had to return to Paris to fill out his claim. Then back he came for another two weeks. Anyway, every other house in Lourdes has a doctor's office, that was one striking thing. But mostly one watches the sick—very brave people. They make the stations of the cross, and that is really an act of penance, for the stations are all outside and one has to travel steep paths to accomplish them. As I remember, Protestants don't have the stations, do they?"

Madame Rogers acknowledged that they didn't. Comparative religions had interested Mme Lucie ever since, she said, her acquaintance with Pastor Weber and his family. She started sorting out the differences in faiths.

"Now Protestants believe that there was a Virgin Mary, but they don't believe that she was immaculate. They have holy communion, but not confirmation." She said it in singsong, as if she were reciting her catechism.

"Well, actually Protestants have both, but communion isn't the same." Madame Lucie started a bit when Mme Rogers explained what communion was in her branch of Protestantism, but then relaxed.

"In any case, we're not so far apart as we used to be. Because of the curé in Caen, I used to think that Protestants were devils. And look, here I am talking to one."

Madame Rogers hadn't grown up with particularly good impressions of Catholics either, and she told Mme Lucie about it. The old woman then declared herself happy that the Church in France was changing.

"When my dear husband died in 1961, I told the funeral director that we couldn't afford more than a third-class funeral and that Pierre would have to be buried in unsanctified ground because of his divorce. 'Don't worry, my poor woman,' he said. He took my papers and arranged everything." She found this a striking change from the attitude of the priest in Lisieux who gave her so much trouble about marrying Pierre.

"He told me to come back after the marriage and he'd see what he could do. In the meantime I was excommunicated and still am. But I can assure you, he's still waiting for me to come back." The funeral director's different attitude had surprised her: maybe the Church could be good to people after all. And whatever the Church said, it was hard for her to believe that so good a man as Pierre was not in heaven. But then, she said gloomily, he hadn't had the sacraments.

Veering toward the problem of the J months, Mme Lucie was on the edge of rehearsing her own despair at Pierre's death. She would often posthumously berate him for sneaking cigarettes even though he had known it was bad for his heart condition. Or she would berate herself for having let them take

[126]

him to the hospital, from which old people never returned. But this time, she continued talking about the Church.

"One difference is that Protestant pastors can marry. I think it's ridiculous that priests can't, don't you?" she asked sensibly.

"Perhaps the Church wants them devoting all their efforts to parishioners and God." The American weakly defended celibacy.

"Well, you may think that happens, but it doesn't. That old cardinal in Lyon died in the arms of a prostitute, and he wasn't the only one. Nature calls, people have their needs, and the priests are all hypocrites. That's why there are so many jokes about them. Papa would come home with a new one every week."

"I've never heard any jokes about priests," Mme Rogers said.

"I'd tell you one, but most of them are risqué. And what would you think of an old woman telling dirty jokes?" Madame Lucie hesitated. Then she decided, "I'll tell one anyway. We're good enough friends for that."

The joke concerned the village curé, his dog, Wurs, and his housekeeper, Marie.

"The housekeeper is always named Marie," Mme Lucie explained. She continued setting the scene: the bishop was suddenly going to pay a visit, the curé wanted Marie to start a good fire for the bishop after his travels, and Marie was worried because the dog, Wurs, was not to be found anywhere. Putting this last problem aside for a moment, Marie rushed to the basement to get an apronful of wood. In the meantime the bishop had arrived.

"Marie came upstairs, her apron loaded with wood, but in her haste and concerned about Wurs, she had pulled her skirt up along with it. (In those days women of the people often didn't wear anything under their long skirts, if you know what I mean.)"

Madame Rogers showed that she understood.

"There was the monseigneur in the hall at the top of the stairs. 'Good evening, *ma fille*,' he managed to say in spite of Marie's bareness. She was wild: 'Oh, Monseigneur, have you seen Wurs?' Looking at her carefully, he replied, 'No, *ma pauvre fille*, I haven't seen worse, but I can assure you I've seen much better.' " Madame Lucie laughed, "It's cute, isn't it?"

Her visitor assured her that it was.

"You weren't offended, were you?"

From then on Mme Lucie began telling stories about curés regularly, and it succeeded in taking their minds off things. Sometimes she could remember the occasion on which her father had brought home a particular story, so that the jokes became intertwined with the tale of her father's business adventures—or misadventures as she reluctantly called them. They passed the month of July that way, until Antoine and Mariette returned from the country with bunches of roses from their garden to cheer her up. Antoine's daily visits resumed, and by September Mme Lucie had regained the equilibrium necessary to deal with the artisans' business.

The business year always revived Mme Lucie's narrative. By late autumn she had discarded her curé jokes for stories of movie stars, show-business personalities, and other celebrities. Having served with her husband as guardian of a movie theater, she knew fifty-year-old gossip about entertainment figures—Mistinguett, Josephine Baker, Fernandel, Charlot, and the great Sarah Bernhardt. She admired Bernhardt partly because she had visited an area in Brittany that memorialized her, and partly because she admired Bernhardt's flair.

"She had many lovers," Mme Lucie informed her visitor, "but she didn't skulk around like some little shopgirl. No—she would brag of her adventures, trying to remember which man she had been with a week before. Was it the Prince of Bavaria or such and such a king or maybe the President of the Republic?"

One wintry evening they reminisced about Harton's water pipes and the feud with Mme Bernard. Madame Rogers commented that Mme Lucie had talent enough to be the President of the Republic herself.

"You're right. My picture on the phonebook cover was just the first step. I can assure you that Monsieur Valéry Giscard d'Estaing won't get another term because people have had it with *gaullisme*. Without further elaboration, she proceeded to give her judgment of all the presidents of France and leading politicians during her lifetime, which she extended back to pre-conception. Sadi-Carnot, who was assassinated on the day her parents married, Félix Faure, who died scandalously—she went through them all.

"Of course, I like René Coty best because he was a Norman. I went to watch him ride through town in his carriage. You could not find a friendlier-looking man." On the list continued. "Pétain saved us, and then De Gaulle paid him back disgracefully. Poor Laval, who gave the French people social security, had to commit suicide so he wouldn't be shot." On those points Mme Lucie remained adamant through years of conversations.

"Now I'm not saying De Gaulle didn't do good things for France. But he was a deserter, and he made our money worthless. One hundred francs are now one; before him, a franc was a franc." In addition, the concierge found the general too aristocratic, a would-be king.

"Pompidou was just the opposite—a man of the people, and the people loved him. Now we have another aristocrat. But I'll tell you, bad as Giscard is, he's better than the Communists. No one in this building would think of voting Communist." She stopped her lesson and refused to say more, except for a few words about her Communist in-laws and their strange ways.

"Well, Mme Lucie, what are we going to do to make you president?"

"I have an idea," she replied playfully. "The concierge union is having a big rally. Maybe I'll go and agitate with them." They both laughed, Mme Lucie because she hated unions, because she couldn't walk as far as the butcher. But

Mme Rogers laughed remembering Harton's description of the concierge in the battle of sixty-eight. Had she wanted to, Mme Lucie *could* machinate to take over anything.

Instead of glory, the old woman settled in that year to the worries of her tenants and family. They, it seemed, brought her only their complaints about cat turds in the hall, cellar lights left on all night, foreigners who didn't obey the law of silence after 10:00 P.M. Over the years the troubles weighed her down, until she was hunched over like a cripple. And sometimes it seemed that her wrinkled face had no space left for another care.

One day, however, her spirits seemed to lift. More happily active than usual, she reported Colette's impending visit to the engineer's family. Madame Lucie speculated on its meaning and was optimistic. Even Colette, she said, was turning sober, having bought a modest black linen suit for the occasion. As the Sunday dinner approached the Passage seemed alert and tense to the possibility of an upwardly mobile marriage in the neighborhood. And when Sunday actually arrived, Colette stopped at the *loge*, as if by instinct, to receive her grandmother's kisses. Pulling the young woman toward her, Mme Lucie pinned one of her mother's brooches to Colette's lapel and sent her off into battle.

That evening, while waiting for news of Colette's triumph, the concierge regaled Mme Rogers with the story of her trip to Caen to find Pierre. Repeating the story seemed to fortify her granddaughter's chances. But as time passed and Colette's footsteps failed to sound in the courtyard, she slipped into her troubles.

"I'm too old for this job. Living on the ground floor is dangerous for someone my age." She told of rappings on her shutters at two in the morning, of passersby whom she could no longer identify.

"I've probably missed Colette tonight just because I can't detect her anymore." The neighborhood, too, frightened her.

"Those little delinquents—Algerians, Arabs, blacks—just mock me when I try to chase them home. All these people from the colonies have no manners, can't even speak French— except for bad words. Sometimes I think I should retire."

Family cares, neighborhood cares, even the cares of old age had often brought a threat of retirement from Mme Lucie. When a threat came, a red alert would pass through the Passage. After four decades of her regime, no one would trust a newcomer with keys. A newcomer would never have Mme Lucie's pull with officials of the arrondissement. How would one know the terms for favors, and who in the mayor's office would give credence to another concierge's signature? In any case, Mme Lucie's threats to retire were always followed by new heights of shuffling energy.

Monday, those following Colette's career were watchful and searching. Madame Perrugia made an extra visit to the *loge* hoping for revelation, but her friend's face betrayed nothing. Madame Lucie could, everyone knew, guard bad tidings or good for weeks. Tenants made the extra visits because at any moment she might break her silence. She might erupt volcanically with the news or coyly invite a visitor into her confidence. For her part, Mme Lucie received the extra ministrations with equanimity—Mme Perrugia asking if she needed anything from the pharmacy, Mme Gourdin suggesting she might want a treat from the bakery. Even Monsieur Robert, the printer, brought her some flowers when he came to fix her eyedrops. After ten days or so the cause appeared futile, and no one dared approach Colette.

The beauty was conducting herself with a grand impassivity, until, at about the same time the solicitation of Mme Lucie stopped, Colette became a font of energy. When she worked days, she returned late in the afternoon with rolls of wallpaper. When on the night shift, she spent her free time carrying parcels and paints to her flat and to the empty one on the floor above. On days off no one saw her except for fleeting moments in a mechanic's jumpsuit, her hair spilling out from a bandana. Something great *was* in the offing; it seemed a dream that so great a personage as an engineer would be moving into the Passage des Chats.

Springtime air and springtime sun filled the tiny street, giving the concierge that lift everyone waited for. Her throat wrapped in an old muffler, she rummaged through her "archives." For Mme Rogers she produced pictures of her dead fiancé, another from her second courtship. She and Pierre were arm in arm, close, young, and smiling.

"I wrote something on the back—what does it say?"

"Souvenir of a beautiful day."

The message was so pure that one could almost feel the simple blessing of the occasion.

"Days are beautiful when one is courting, the most beautiful days, in fact." Madame Lucie's remark seemed a clue to Colette's activity.

"And look at this old muffler. Can you believe I made it for Pierre before he had to return to the war, before he was sent to Salonika?" The muffler, though battered, seemed as eternal as Mme Lucie herself.

"Now here's a scrap of fabric from a silk foulard of his. That I made when we ran the theater in Courbevoie. Pierre had to wear a smoking jacket to greet the moviegoers—things were so much more elegant then. Today all they wear are jeans, jeans, always blue jeans."

"Did he wear out that scarf?" Mme Rogers asked, fingering the fragile white silk.

"Not at all. It disappeared. Only years later did I find out that Philippe had borrowed it without his father's permission when he was courting Nanette. At a fair in Neuilly he lost it on a roller coaster." The scarf had bound Antoine and Philippe in a conspiracy of guilt, Antoine always threatening to tell the secret should he not have his own way. Madame Lucie continued making piles of souvenirs and photographs, trinkets and scraps of paper.

"Now look at this little child. She's cute, isn't she? There I am in my brown plaid dress—I must have worn it four or five years, because that's how many times I remember Maman letting the hem down. And here we both are. Look at our sausage curls. My mother knew every trick there was with hair and hats."

Madame Lucie was looking tired, so her friend suggested putting things away before Antoine's arrival.

"No, we'll just sit and talk a bit more. We can't have our usual visit tonight because Colette's bringing the baby around. You know, she's very sad after her great deception."

It all became clear. The more active Colette was, the more it was a matter of pride hiding defeat.

"Yes, she does look busy, but not happy. Her young man's family had heard nothing about the baby until the Sunday she visited them. I guess they threatened to cut him off if he became engaged. So it's finished."

"And Colette is taking her mind off it all by redecorating," Mme Rogers continued the story. "Everyone thought she was getting her place ready for a new husband."

Madame Lucie shifted in her chair. "No, *ma petite dame*. In fact she's fixing an apartment for my retirement—in a few weeks. That's why we're sorting out all my souvenirs."

6

Madame Lucie Retired

Summer 1981

The first months after Mme Lucie's departure amounted to a prolonged nuisance for some of the tenants of the building. Madame Bernard reacted by further elevating her nose as she picked her way through the debris that had begun to gather in the entryways. The artisans had a difficult time hauling their burdens through the tricycles, wagons, and assorted toys that mingled with the litter. Less physically hard-pressed, Monsieur Robert, the printer, and Dubois, the chair merchant, acted as if nothing had happened, even while they dodged the small children who belonged to the toys and to the new concierge.

Madame Rogers, absent during the transition, returned to the Passage romantically expecting to find the old Napoleonic stones a heap of rubble. So she was disappointed that the sun still shone, chairs still passed through the archway, and young men still watched for Colette from their doorways. Even Harton's response to the situation was predictable.

"What a woman that new concierge is," he exulted. "Three kids under six, not one of them is legitimate, and not one, I wager, has the same father." It was true that the children looked like an advertisement for UNICEF.

"Carmen, I call her—the only woman I ever met who was raised on the Rue de Lappe. She's not a person to tangle with." Harton, it seemed, had changed his position on the infamous street and was now allowing its reputation to stand.

About thirty years old, Carmen had the special vigor of a stout young woman. Her dress was frowsy, her language tough, and her manners were 1960s instead of *belle époque*. Of Spanish descent, she represented the new underclasses of the Faubourg St. Antoine. As she bustled coarsely through the courtyard, yelling at children, pushing orange peels into corners with her feet, Carmen's presence—depending on one's point of view— either confirmed Mme Lucie's dignity or testified to the eternal ignominy of being a concierge. Madame Lucie herself took a clear stand on the issue: she never again descended to the ground floor.

Instead, she sat in her new one-room flat, knitting strips only to tear them out again when the ball of yarn was finished. Her easy chair was placed back to the door, facing across the bed to the window where Kiki the canary sang in his cage. Pigeons visited the ledge every day, less often to see Kiki than to peck at the rice Mme Lucie had illegally left for them. She had always favored these "poor little beasts," and now, perched high herself, could indulge them as she wished.

"Things have certainly changed in the *loge*, haven't they?" she had commented on Mme Rogers's first visit. All her news and all the praise for her past contributions now came by repeatedly asking this question.

But Mme Rogers had been too busy looking at the new arrangement of Mme Lucie's life to give a winning answer. What she saw gave her pause. Colette had covered the walls with garish orange-flowered wallpaper, as if in defiance of the proper bourgeois family that had rejected her. From her former life Mme Lucie had kept the yellow-flowered drapes and bedspread

and the red oilcloth tablecloth. Though the pictures of Saint
Theresa and the children, the armoire stocked with archives,
were still in evidence, the hot colors seemed a strange contrast
to the concierge's cold hands and shuffled gait. Walking more
slowly than ever, Mme Lucie reached out for walls, table, and
chairs to support and guide her. Retirement had released her
from fortitude.

Sitting there, she had told Mme Rogers how the concierge's
job had changed. "That little woman is very courageous, but she
doesn't know how to do anything except have babies. She told
me she's pregnant again."

The new concierge had wisely developed a rapport with her
predecessor, and Mme Lucie took some comfort in that. She
had even gone so far as to counsel Carmen to have an abortion,
advice she apparently took. The younger woman had also told
her about life on the Rue de Lappe.

"Just what I expected. She's not French, you know. Most of
the new concierges aren't."

Madame Lucie's voice was colorless, and it shocked her
friend to hear it so. Too much had changed and was still
changing. Across the street in the modern buildings, the concierge had been converted into a *gardien* who held another job
and from his apartment on the second floor merely kept an eye
out that all went well. Mail deliveries were being cut back, only
a couple each day. So there was no sense in having a full-time
person to tend to that.

"Anyway, this one downstairs won't last long, you mark my
words." As usual Mme Lucie's prediction turned out to be
accurate. In little more than a year the *loge* had been trans-
formed, painted white and stripped of all furniture and people
except for a desk. Incongruous in the old building, it looked like
a modern office.

"Madame Paul, the paperhanger's wife, is taking care of
things now. She goes down a few times a day to do the mail—
that's all." The situation seemed more an indictment of Mme

Lucie's forty years of service than Carmen had been.

"Well, Mme Lucie," her friend said, "I for one am glad she's in charge of taking care of you and keeping you out of trouble. What mischief have you been up to while I've been gone?" Madame Rogers wanted her old friend back, wanted stories and action, the archives pulled out, and memories recalled.

"Nothing, just nothing. I can't walk, I can't see, and everybody has to do everything for me." She set her chin, refusing to be amusing or amused.

"Somebody's working hard. Your apartment looks so tidy."

"That's because the *mairie* sends a helper three times a week to do my shopping and a little cleaning." Even that failed to lift her spirits. Three days a week, three hours a day wasn't enough time to do all the necessary cleaning. In the summer when the helpers took vacations, the personnel was unreliable. Sometimes it would be a Senegalese, the next time someone different.

"This week it's a real French woman, very nice, but she can't do more than run the dustmop around a bit."

Madame Lucie's moods alternated between torpor and crankiness. When the latter set in, no one could please her. Friends who visited either stayed too long, talked too loud, or didn't understand her problems. Those who failed to come had forgotten her or were disloyal. At other times waves of depression flooded her conversation.

"Have you ever visited Père Lachaise cemetery, Madame?"

Madame Rogers had but wondered aloud why Mme Lucie was interested.

"Did I tell you my poor parents are buried there? The one good deed of my Aunt Suzanne, because only Parisians or their relatives can find a place. But I haven't been able to tend their graves in years. Just like everything else. Maybe they've been vandalized, maybe disappeared even."

Madame Rogers knew this as an opening that had to be

investigated, so she volunteered that some week she might be going that way.

"Their graves are in fact not too far from that of Planquette. Have I told you about him?—he was Norman and wrote plays. I saw them as a child with Maman, and Mme Planquette knit Aunt Suzanne a baby cap when my grandparents had their bakery in Trouville. Just ask the guardian where Planquette is buried."

It sounded easy enough, or maybe impossible.

"Then Edith Piaf—do you know about her?—she's not too far away. Oh yes, and one more. Very close by is the monument of a famous monsieur whose name I forget. In any case, in the sculpture of him nothing is hidden."

A sudden flash of the old humor was intriguing enough to send Mme Rogers out until she found Planquette, Piaf, and finally the monument to Oscar Wilde. She searched diligently for "a stone monument topped by an iron cross enclosed by an iron grill." Several nearby graves were in fact in such a state of disarray with markers, bits of wrought iron, and urns was strewn about that no indication remained of who lay buried there. Yet it hardly mattered in one sense, for Mme Lucie never broached the subject again. Instead of crankiness and depression, more and more a general lassitude swallowed the old woman up. Staring into space, her hands folded across the neglected knitting, she could not be roused to conversation or, it seemed, to life. So Mme Rogers wasn't surprised, only frightened, when a few days later at the usual visiting hour she found the apartment door carelessly left open and no sign of Mme Lucie.

She knocked nonetheless, and from behind the open door, standing at the stove in the corner, the helper gave out the bad news.

"Madame Lemaire isn't well today, and I've called the doctor," she said in a booming voice. She explained that she would stay and cook some soup until the doctor came to relieve her. Then a feeble call from the sickbed.

"Is that the American? I want to see her."

For the first time since the old woman's retirement, Mme Rogers felt momentarily relieved. Despite Mme Lucie's miserable appearance, she could still identify a passerby. Her condition was nevertheless alarming, hands hot with fever, pain in her abdomen, and the loud voice of the helper inflaming the atmosphere. Earnest and good-natured, the "real Frenchwoman" of a helper stood making soup for her patient, all the while bellowing out words of reassurance.

"I've had lots of old women—my grandmothers I call them—sick before. Only a few of them died on me." She proceeded to give the recipe for the soup and an account of all the sick old people it had cured. Again she repeated that in very few cases had it failed to heal the patient.

"Don't worry, Mme Lemaire," she said, "I'll stay here all night to keep you company if you need it."

Madame Lucie thanked her feebly, but then her voice solidified. "There really is no need for you to wear yourself out now. I've got the American here so you can go home to your family. You're a good woman, and the *mairie* will certainly hear about all the good things you've done for me." In a flash the helper was gone, having loudly promised to return in the morning.

"My but she's tiring, although when she's around I do feel less afraid about falling asleep and not waking up." She asked Mme Rogers politely if she would mind staying with her while she took a little nap. Once her visitor had taken up her own knitting, Mme Lucie went to sleep until a knock sounded at the door almost an hour later.

"Doctor Posta is out of town and I'm his replacement," a tiny young woman announced to Mme Rogers. She marched into the sickroom, giving orders as she went for the American to sit in the kitchen and for Mme Lucie to adjust her clothing for an examination. One could hear the covers rustling and Mme Lucie breathing hard as she moved.

"Doctoress, how good of you to come. Am I going to die! You can tell me the truth." The moment she had been waiting for and feared had finally arrived.

"You're certainly going to have to wait until I examine you for an answer, Mme Lemaire." As she examined, she questioned.

"How old are you, Madame?"

"Eighty-five. Do you think I look that old?" The doctoress refused the chance to compliment and proceeded with more questions about Mme Lucie's body. Another knock at the door and Antoine appeared, greeting Mme Rogers with a handshake and a motion toward the bed.

"How's she doing?" he asked with unusual anxiety. The American pointed to the doctoress and then excused herself. She had been rescued from an indeterminate guard duty over the medical profession. Now Antoine could protect his mother from what she really feared—being sent to the hospital and a certain death. He could also receive instructions for food and medicine. Most important from Mme Lucie's point of view, Antoine would witness the doctoress in person and see in fact that his mother was sicker than Mariette.

By late the next morning Mme Lucie's apartment was grandly stocked with pharmaceutical products, written medical orders, and visitors. Having done more cooking, the helper was about to leave. In the guest's chair Mme Perrugia sat entertaining Mme Lucie with conversations about the sick and dying in the neighborhood. The concierge seemed happy for another newcomer to whom she could explain, if only weakly, her own condition, which was really the issue at hand.

"The doctoress says I have a microbe in my intestine. That's what's giving me the fever." She had strength for little more, so Mme Perrugia continued her stories.

Madame Lucie made a slow recovery, but within a few days she could at least describe her treatment—three different kinds of medicine and a restricted diet. Madame Perrugia, whose visits now seemed to coincide with Mme Rogers's, jumped in with a description of an intestinal infection she had once suffered. Feeling better, Mme Lucie countered with further instructions:

"I have to take my temperature morning and afternoon, with a half hour of rest before the afternoon measurement. In fact, I think I'll take my nap now." And she shut her eyes tightly.

It was a signal to leave, so both women rose and said good-bye. Madame Lucie opened one eye.

"Maybe you'd better stay, Mme Rogers. Then I won't be afraid of dying. Help Mme Perrugia to the door first; she's having trouble with her leg."

When they reached the door, the women shook hands, Mme Perugia adjusted her cane and stepped out into the hall.

"I'm going to get some rest myself, and don't think I can't use it, what with Mme Lucie calling me every hour to tell me she's about to die." Madame Perrugia was angry that the concierge's whims always took precedence over every other concern. Over eighty herself, she did her own shopping, took the initiative to see friends.

"Between the two of us, Mme Lucie likes being sick and making the world jump through her hoop." The indictment was interrupted by a call from the sickbed. So Mme Rogers quickly said another good-bye and hurried back in.

Madame Lucie tried to suppress her annoyance. "I must have my rest and can't get it with the two of you talking in the hall."

Now Mme Rogers was annoyed herself. The gross manipulation made her want to rebel like Colette, to lecture Mme Lucie the way Antoine did, or at least complain like Mme Perrugia to someone else. But a prisoner by the fact that she was neither family nor eighty years old, she sat down, vowing to leave as soon as the half hour was up.

After twenty minutes Mme Lucie asked if the time had passed.

"Exactly," Mme Rogers lied. "You must have a clock inside your head. And I guess I'd better be on my way too."

"You're going to desert me just when I need you to read the thermometer?" Madame Lucie's voice grew faint as she seemed to fall back into deep sickness. Eighty-five, almost blind, wrinkled, now feverish, and in reality, perhaps dying—what kind of armor of experience did it take to turn one's back on her?

"I guess I can stay a little longer. I just thought you might need a real nap."

"The thermometer is in the drawer. Make sure you shake it down well." She then instructed the American to sit in the kitchen while she put the thermometer in.

"You are truly my savior—nobody else takes care of me the way you do."

In the tiny kitchen fronting the main room and separated from it by a half wall and window, Mme Rogers felt like a bad child. She sat on a low stool, her back to the window that would have allowed her to watch the old woman take her temperature rectally. One part of her said that she should leave, for Mme Lucie would certainly find Mariette, Irène, or some other tenant to read the thermometer, so great was her experience in command and manipulation. The other part, however, made her realize how much energy it took Mme Lucie just to stay alive. In fact, it was her sole occupation at the moment and one that gave only an ambiguous satisfaction. Succeeding at that task released energy for nothing but complaints.

"It's ready," Mme Lucie called, and while the thermometer was being read she explained how she counted to two hundred to judge the time.

"Thirty-seven point five, almost normal," was the verdict.

"Still, it's a fever. Now I'll call up the doctor to report."

Madame Lucie Retired

She asked Mme Rogers to dial the number. It was written in digits about five inches tall on a paper by the phone. One could chart the deterioration of Mme Lucie's eyes in the increasing size of important telephone numbers. No more than an inch high a decade before, they were now enormous and wavy, signaling also the old woman's loss of motor control. As the number rang, Mme Rogers passed the receiver.

"Hello, doctoress? It's me. I still have a fever, thirty-seven point five." The conversation proceeded with a description of symptoms she had had four days before and of those that remained. She rehearsed the medicines and the schedule for taking them.

"I'll call you tomorrow at the same time. No, I want to call you anyway. It makes me feel better. Good-bye, doctoress."

"How did she think you are doing?"

"Very well. I think I'll call Sister Marie-Ste. Geneviève. No, you stay here, please." She motioned her visitor back to the chair and then, changing her mind, asked her to dial the convent. After talking to several intermediaries, Mme Lucie finally reached the sister.

"Sister, it's me. I'm in bed with an infection in my intestines." She repeated the conversation of five minutes before.

"No, the little American is with me. Yes, Sister. Thank you, Sister, you are too good to me. Good-bye, Sister." Madame Lucie had a small smile on her face, as she lay back on her pillow. "She's going to come to see me tomorrow. I think I'll give her a small bottle of champagne." Madame Lucie began praising the work of the sisters for the neighborhood, both by keeping the dispensary open and by visiting the sick at home. She assured Mme Rogers that they would even help Protestants and Arabs who were moving into the area.

Madame Rogers grew interested, for it seemed that Mme Lucie might be on the verge of reminiscing. As long as the octogenarian memory was at work, she herself felt some sort of reason for staying.

"You know the sisters are human like us. They have their little celebrations; they even have their little quarrels and vanities. I've heard, for example, that Sister Hélène has a temper and that she and another sister don't get on too well. It reminds me of any other neighborhood argument, like those of Mariette who's always vexed with one person or another, and of course, they feel the same about her. You've noticed that Mariette hasn't bothered to spend any time with me since I've been sick. It's terrible to be old and neglected by one's own daughter-in-law."

"What do the sisters have to do to belong to their order?" Mme Rogers asked. But Mme Lucie would have nothing to do with that topic now that she had stumbled on the villainies of Mariette.

"I need my medicine. You see the packet on the table?" and she continued with instructions for preparing the packet's contents in a small glass of water.

Unaccustomed to spending her visits with Mme Lucie in such a way, Mme Rogers grew increasingly angry with this preoccupation with the body and its incessant malfunctioning. Madame Lucie, she felt, was becoming like a small child, but one who successfully achieved her ends. Her vision was limited to herself, her world was getting smaller and definitely less interesting. For the next week, however, the ritual of sickness and medicine continued. So did the temperature-taking with Mme Rogers sequestered in the kitchen and then dialing the doctor to report that the temperature was normal. As she grew stronger, the old woman fortified the ritual itself by adding another procedure. Madame Rogers was to record the evening temperature on a piece of paper next to the morning report (who had done that? she wondered). Then both were recited and compared to the figures for the preceding day to the uninterested doctoress.

Madame Perrugia also grew impatient, never more so than the day when she was requested to stay for the temperature-taking.

Madame Lucie Retired

"Why do we have to go into the kitchen?" she protested.

"You have to, that's all. This isn't the Folies Bergère."

Madame Rogers led the way and sat down with her back to the main room. Madame Perrugia followed sulkily.

"She's under the covers. I don't see why we have to be displaced like this for that Madame Pompadour. And me with my bad leg." Then, with a harrumph, Mme Perrugia planted her cane on the floor, lifted herself from the seat she had just taken, and looked through the window in rebellion.

"Why—she puts the thermometer in from the front, not the back. From the front! If she'd put it in from the back we wouldn't have to leave." She left the kitchen and accused Mme Lucie insultingly of being less than stupid.

The old concierge yelped. "Now you've upset me. Now I have to start all over again with another half hour of rest, the thermometer shaken down, and Mme Rogers will have to sit here for the whole thing. And she has a family waiting for her." She motioned to Mme Perrugia, "You might as well go home and get some rest yourself." Her politeness almost failed as she dismissed the sturdy old woman.

"Madame Lucie, don't you think you could skip taking your temperature this afternoon? Perhaps if you sat in the chair you'd feel like your old self again."

"I couldn't do it. I'm too weak, and now I'm angry on top of it," she whined.

"That's because your muscles are deteriorating from not being used."

"I promise I'll try tomorrow. Anyway, we can't take my temperature because it's time for my powdered medicine. Could you put a little less water in it today?" When the mixture was prepared, Mme Lucie drank it down, looking, Mme Rogers thought to herself, like the proverbial "good girl." But whose regime was the old woman obeying?

Only when taking her medicine could Mme Lucie muster any decorum. As soon as she had downed it, her petulance returned, charging Mme Perrugia with a lack of understanding for people less strong and less healthy than herself. Depressed by the concierge's lack of charity, Mme Rogers thought of how to excuse herself from further visits. They had become more of a duty than a delight. But in reaching that conclusion it struck her that she was seeing Mme Lucie from her children's point of view. Bound to her by a biological cord, they heard her physical complaints, were called upon to serve her physical needs, and resorted to evasions to save themselves. Yet Mme Rogers was not a relative, and visiting was not her duty. The next day, still wondering why she went, she knocked at the apartment at the regular time and to her surprise found Mme Lucie sitting in her chair. She had even returned to her usual custom of drinking a Banania toward the end of the day.

"How do you think I look?"

"You look much better, especially sitting up."

"I guess I was too hard on Mme Perrugia yesterday," she said repentantly. "She's had a difficult life—she deserves her trips."

"But it's nice for you, too. She can bring you all the news."

Madame Lucie acknowledged that her old friend always had a little report from the neighborhood. Seeming to forget herself, she reiterated her own point about Mme Perrugia's suffering. Born in Pisa, she had moved with her husband to France in the twenties, when life had been difficult in Italy. Almost straightaway she had settled in the Passage des Chats, and no sooner there, she had lost her two little daughters in an epidemic of diphtheria. Or was it scarlet fever? Madame Lucie couldn't remember which.

"Then the poor thing lost her husband. Well, Mme Perrugia just picked herself up and started cleaning apartments to earn a living. So I guess she's earned her club meetings and bus tours." Madame Lucie explained to her foreign guest that Jacques Chirac, the mayor of Paris, had instituted trips on the Seine and set up leisure programs for older citizens. Madame Perrugia, she said, had been first in line for all of them.

Madame Lucie Retired

Suddenly Mme Lucie stopped herself and thought out loud.

"But what good does it do, all this talk about the past?" She searched for another topic and started in on politics.

"I have to admit that Monsieur Chirac at least kept his promises to old people like us. Now this new man—Mitterrand—he's made too many promises to be able to keep any of them. Miracles, that's what he says. But what does he do first thing in office? He goes to the Panthéon and puts flowers on all the tombs—just like any politician. In a year or so we're going to have lots of babies names François or Françoise after him—that's no miracle either."

Madame Lucie spoke from experience, but bitterness now edged even the humor in her remarks. Besides, she decided, she didn't want to talk politics either.

"That's all anyone can talk about. In the old days we discussed everything else and politics very little. My husband and I never discussed who we were voting for, even with each other. Now you can't escape it—on the radio, on television. It's just more entertainment, instead of a dignified decision about voting."

Not the past, not politics, nothing in the return of her volubility gave Mme Lucie solace. Everything she was used to reporting turned sour. Talking about the family was worse. She had seen Colette this morning only because the young woman's arms were laden with packages and she wanted to leave things in her grandmother's apartment. Accompanying her, Mme Lucie said, were two disagreeable men, one of them her current beau.

"He's an ecologist. I've just found out what that means. They go to the Forest of Fontainebleau to change the oil in his car."

During this bedridden period Antoine had sat at his mother's side for longer than usual spells. One could tell by his look that he was worried, until he too became exasperated by her self-imposed failure to rally. But during the first few days he filled the silence her sickness left with every bit of family news he could think of. As usual with the younger Lemaires, some of it was happy, some tempestuous. Now that she had time to chew it over before Mme Rogers, however, everything came out as if infected with the decay of her body.

"Antoine says that Mariette has suddenly decided to love their country home. Can you believe that!" Madame Rogers had already heard this from Mariette herself when they met one day in the street. Discussing their July holiday, she had beamed with pleasure. Maybe, she said, an end to house renovations had allowed them time to relax and enjoy the place. Before, it had been a burden, loading the car with tools, paint, plaster, and all the supplies necessary to refurbishing what had been a rotting building.

"Every time I think of that place," Mme Lucie continued, "it frightens me. Why did Antoine buy a house in Picardy where the armies always invade?"

The late afternoon August sun made the small apartment like a furnace. Outside a young man was fixing a motorcycle, and loud rock music from his radio filled the small passage and the even smaller apartment. For the first time in the decade that Mme Rogers had visited her, Mme Lucie said that she had to use the toilet. Her toilet was a chamberpot, emptied every other day by the helper from the *mairie*. It now sat, Mme Rogers suddenly realized, right in the middle of the room.

"You go into the kitchen, and I'll call you when I'm finished." Returning, she found the old woman hobbling around the room, her underwear at her ankles. She sat down without pulling it up, all pride gone.

"And now, worst of all, we have Simone in town. She has left her husband." Pained, but driven by some compulsion to reveal the bad news, she told how Simone's husband had abused her, how the housewife who had never done an adventurous deed in her life had packed up her belongings and the one child who happened to be at home with her that day and set out for Paris.

"Her husband's a mailman and in thick with the police. So she couldn't get them to help her have the other child released from school." So the boy who wanted to become an archeologist was left with his father in Simone's escape. Madame Lucie was comforted that Colette had shown some worth by immediately finding her sister a job in the Métro.

"But the Métro! Think of the people she'll meet there, like Jean-Claude or Colette's horrible friend Jacqueline, who's a loose woman of the first order."

But most of all Mme Lucie worried about the boy left at home with a man she considered a monster. Absorbing all of Simone's shame and horror, she described what the mailman-husband had supposedly done, sordid things that fit a pornographic nightmare. She could not, she confessed, bear to think about the cruel reality of Simone's apparently idyllic marriage. But the images would not retreat. They haunted her.

"There's something else I haven't told you. I've been having hallucinations."

Madame Rogers didn't understand. The idea was too preposterous.

"I'll see a woman, for example, and she'll have a mustache and rabbit ears. Or vultures will come flying through the window and settle in the apartment. I don't know what it means."

No one could help with the problem, not the doctor who humored her, not Antoine who passed it off as a play for attention. More than her other infirmities, the hallucinations isolated her from normal sociability. And they frightened her with their unpredictability and their portent of worse to come.

Madame Rogers was no help either. In the last year she too had developed a standard response to Mme Lucie's ill humor of any sort. Treating her like a child, she tried to divert attention from the problem at hand by asking an irrelevant question about the past. It always involved some point on which Mme Lucie had previously expounded at great length. Hats, for example, often set the old woman talking for half an hour, so Mme Rogers would pretend to have forgotten what a napoleon was, or a charlotte. Caen, or Normandy in general, was a favorite topic, and the year before Mme Rogers had toured all the landmarks of Mme Lucie's life. That had provided them with a week of conversations. Because songs could also set the old woman into a reverie of humming and recitations, Mme Rogers determined to try that tack this evening. Having listened to the story of the mailman-monster and the hallucinations, she should have been more prepared for Mme Lucie's answer, but she wasn't.

"You know, Mme Lucie, sometimes I think about writing a little history of growing up in Caen during the *belle epoque*."

The old woman failed to stir. Her visitor went on to explain that she couldn't remember the song that people sang when the soldiers marched back to the garrison. "C'est la faute d'amour," she thought it was. No response.

Madame Lucie folded her arms and grimly bowed her head.

"Remember how you told me about your parents not being able to find you, how you would sit on the baker boy's shoulders and watch the torchlight procession?"

The old woman remained silent a few seconds more, but she was too polite to ignore her visitor.

"I can't sing it. I used to love to sing, but I can't sing for you anymore. It makes me too sad to sing or to think about the past."

It now became clear that during the past few weeks Mme Lucie had reached the end of memory. In the depths of old age, present and future prospects had disappeared from her perspective on life, so she lost sight of the past. She had been jarred by Simone's troubles, overwhelmed by her own eerie visions to the point that she had lost her sense of time. Like the Duc de Guermantes, she had been wobbling, for the past few weeks, on the cliffs of memory. Now she had lost her footing and was clinging for safety's sake to the one thing she knew existed—her feeble, aged body.

Preoccupation with physical being seemed unfortunate, for the memory Mme Lucie now rejected had been her context, indeed her very life. It had pulsated with the accent of experience before she refused it. Stretching her youth and her origins, memory had sweetened old age with revivals of her parents, reconstructions of Philippe and Pierre, and recitations of old pleasures. It was also a personal fantasy, as Mme Rogers was slowly discovering, whose factual basis was sometimes subtly altered for greater aesthetic affect or for personal satisfaction. Saint Theresa had not died the day Mme Lucie was born; Pierre Laval had been shot after the liberation of France, though he tried to commit suicide. Depending on which two events Mme Lucie wanted to coincide the dates for the marriage of her parents, the death of Sadi-Carnot, and the birth of Michel could have occurred alternately on June 22, 23, or 24. Even Pierre, the good husband, surrendered his reality to her need for a spouse six, eleven, or twelve years her senior.

Without memory this unique identity was slipping away and with it Mme Lucie's decades as concierge, charged with local import, characters, bustle, and the lore of neighborhoods and generations. How sad to see them go the way of the Rue Marché au Beurre, which had disappeared from Lisieux, to disintegrate as had her parents' tomb. One wanted to save this witness to France, this confession, this history, before they evaporated; one wanted to bring Mme Lucie back to life. The only solution was to help recapture the past for her.

NOTES AND ACKNOWLEDGMENTS

Madame Lucie told this story of her life in bits and pieces, without chronology, and often without names. To construct a coherent narrative I followed her footsteps throughout France and checked her memories in the pages of French history and in archives. What I found were errors and what I assume were deliberate bits of misremembering. For example, René Viviani probably inaugurated the savings bank in Caen in 1906, when he was minister of labor and social welfare. For Mme Lucie, however, this was a pre-school occurrence rather than one that took place when she was ten. More interesting is the dating of Saint Theresa's death to coincide with Mme Lucie's birth and of Sadi-Carnot's assassination to coincide with her parent's marriage, which in turn was often moved to coincide with the birth of Michel. I have left these and other misrememberings: *Caveat lector*. In addition, most names in this account have been changed and so has the precise location of the Passage des Chats as well as its precise name.

Because this book evolved over fifteen years, many people have contributed to its completion. Obviously, Mme Lucie was its inspiration. Her neighbors Barbara and Pierre Allemand, Rosemary and W. Albert Duaime, and Charlotte and Al Kessler provided the proper ambience for thinking and writing about her. Among my colleagues here and in France Mary Young, Judy Diner, William Leach, Sanford Elwitt, Christopher Lasch, Françoise McCreary, Eugene McCreary, Nancy Lyman Roelker, and Carole Vopat have offered special encouragement, criticism, and—like Mme Lucie herself—inspiration. Peter Agree shared the insights and information of his research into the nature of oral history. Patience Smith, Patrick Smith, and Robert J. Smith gave expert testimony about Mme Lucie. Jean DeGroat and Helen Hull not only typed several versions of this manuscript; they also offered the first critique. Charles Grench and Michael Joyce of Yale University Press worked that manuscript and all its eccentricities into a book.

Donald Kelley, who constantly questioned my interest in Mme Lucie, helped my visits to her to become a story. Encouraging the degree of historical iconoclasm this book represents, he is (nonetheless) my model historian and my best-loved reader.

Index

Index

CPSIA information can be obtained
at www.ICGtesting.com
Printed in the USA
FSHW011359291221
87273FS